THE COVENANT AND THE KINGDOM

The Covenant and the Kingdom

A Way Through the
Old Testament: II

Joshua, Judges, Samuel and Kings

by

JOSEPH RHYMER

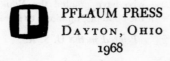

PFLAUM PRESS
DAYTON, OHIO
1968

First Published 1968
Sheed and Ward Ltd, 33 Maiden Lane, London W.C.2 and
Sheed and Ward Pty Ltd, 95 York Street, Sydney

Library of Congress Catalog Card Number: 68-22895

Nihil Obstat: LIONEL SWAIN, S.T.L., L.S.S.

Imprimatur: ✠ PATRICK CASEY, VICAR-GENERAL
Westminster, 22 November 1967

Printed in the U. S. A.

To Anthony and Ruth Humphreys

Contents

Introduction   1

1 Canaan, the promised land   5
2 The people of the covenant   23
3 The judges   41
4 Saul   57
5 The young David   75
6 The crisis of kingship   93
7 Solomon   111
8 The pattern of redemption   129

Maps and diagrams

   Main Canaanite cities and road system   20

   The pattern of redemption   145

Index of names and subjects   147

Introduction

FROM 1164 TO 945 BC there is a gap in the Egyptian records of their conquests and activities in Palestine and the Lebanon. From 1076 to 833 BC there is a gap in the Assyrian accounts of their campaigns in the same area at the eastern end of the Mediterranean. The two gaps overlap by a period of just over a hundred and thirty years: 1076 to 945 BC.

There would be nothing remarkable about this if it were not for one fact which finds no mention in any of the Egyptian or Assyrian documents that have so far been discovered. Between 1030 and 931 BC the Hebrew people changed their form of government from a loose federation of scattered tribes to a highly organised monarchy, and carved out an empire which controlled or dominated the whole area from the Lebanese mountains to the Egyptian border. This book is about the three kings, Saul, David, and Solomon, who occupied the Hebrew throne during those years.

Although there is no mention of the Hebrew people in the records of the great powers of the time, all the accounts mention one area of interest, insignificant at first sight, but sufficient to enable our minds to bridge the gaps between the nations and to obtain a point of entry into their lives. The Assyrian king Tiglath Pileser I, who lived from 1114 to 1076 BC, records:

I went to the Lebanon, and cut timber of cedars for the temple of Anu and Adad, the great gods, my lords, and carried them to Ashur.

And the first Assyrian king after the gap, Ashurnasipal II, who lived from 883 to 859 BC, records:

I seized the entire extent of the Lebanon mountain and reached the Great Sea of the Amurru country (the Mediterranean). I cleaned my weapons in the deep sea and performed sheep-offerings to the gods. . . . I ascended the mountains of the Amanus (the range to the north of the Lebanon) and cut down logs of cedar . . . for the construction of a sanctuary for the temples of Sin and Shamash, the light-giving gods. [J. B. Pritchard, *Ancient Near Eastern Texts*, Princeton University Press, 1955, 275f.]

The same theme runs in the Egyptian texts: three hundred and fifty-one pieces of cedar—slabs, beams, and logs—for the temples at Thebes, Memphis, and various less important places.

David and Solomon obtained their cedar by trade agreements and the gifts of courtesy between kings, but it nevertheless puts them in the same picture as the powers whose reputations are so much more impressive:

[2]

Hiram king of Tyre [the main city of the Lebanon at this time] sent envoys to David with cedar wood and carpenters and stonemasons, who built David a palace. [2 Sm 5:11]

And:

And Hiram sent word to Solomon, 'I have received your message. For my part, I will supply all you want in the way of cedar wood and juniper. Your servants will bring these down from Lebanon to the sea, and I shall have them towed by sea to any place you name; I shall discharge them there and you will take them over. For your part, you will see to the provisioning of my household as I direct.' So Hiram provided Solomon with all the cedar wood and juniper he wanted, while Solomon gave Hiram twenty thousand kors of wheat to feed his household, and twenty thousand kors of pure oil. Solomon gave Hiram this every year. [1 K 5:22-26]

We may have to treat the quantities mentioned with a certain amount of caution, for a kor was a hundred gallons, but there is no need to doubt the existence of the trade agreement.

The root problems of government are the same everywhere and at all times: the relationship between the individual and the organisation, between the bureaucratic structure and the people. When the government is an avowed theocratic which claims to rule in the name of God, and the theology is one which places an infinite value on the person of the individual citizen, the experiences of failure and of success become relevant and important to our own situation. But in addition, the

[3]

concepts formed during this period of David and Solomon, concepts of kingship, wisdom, prophecy, and the implications of the covenant between God and his people, were used to penetrate into the mystery of the redemptive activity of God and the climax this activity reached in the life and work of Jesus Christ. They are concepts which we still turn to in our theology, the liturgy, and our personal devotions. They were used by the people who crowded round Jesus Christ as he entered Jerusalem in triumph at the beginning of the week before his death and resurrection:

And those who went in front and those who followed were all shouting, '*Hosanna! Blessings on him who comes in the name of the Lord!* Blessings on the coming kingdom of our father David! *Hosanna* in the highest heavens!' [Mk 11:9-10]

They recur at the beginning of the most solemn moments of the Mass, and we use them whenever we pray, 'Lord, have mercy'. We can gain much by exploring the period when the concepts were coined.

Kersham
Christmas 1967

Canaan, the Promised Land

JUST BEFORE it reaches Haifa, where the ridge of Mount Carmel juts into the sea, one branch of the great coast road points inland to the northeast. If you have travelled up the road, you have already passed through towns, or the remains of towns, which have been there for more than four thousand years, for this is the ancient road from Egypt to another main cradle of civilisation, Mesopotamia, and it keeps as close to the sea as the shifting sand and patches of salt swamp will permit. The fork in the road below Haifa climbs over the ridge of Mount Carmel and drops into the valley of Jezreel. Less than twelve miles away, on the far side of the valley, is Nazareth, and to the right the land falls away into the valley of the river Jordan. But the main centre of interest is the isolated, flattopped hill which stands to the left of the road on the edge of the ridge you have just passed over, for this is the remains of a town where over twenty separate layers of occupation have been uncovered. It is

Megiddo, the guardian fortress of the valley of Jezreel, the stronghold which protected a whole complex of little villages and which provided a well-provisioned shelter to which the local people could flee when enemies flooded into their valley. When the Hebrews crossed the Jordan and infiltrated the land which they claimed God had given to them, Megiddo was one of the towns, already ancient, which they failed to take over for several generations.

On the top of the hill of Megiddo, you stand on the debris of many different peoples who have occupied this site in their turn and built on the levelled ruins of those who had occupied it before them. The archaeologists of our own times, who have excavated the site and told us the story of the city's history, have left sections of their work open. The most impressive part of the ruins is the great complex of the gateway and the massive walls which stretch out from it; the huge blocks of stone breathe an air of complete assurance, of a people proud of their achievement and security, and confident of their ability to maintain it. For this is just one of the many places which Solomon fortified and used as a provincial centre for the administration of his kingdom, just as the medieval kings of England made their presence felt throughout the country with a network of castles:

King Solomon raised a levy throughout Israel for forced labour: the levy numbered thirty thousand men. . . . Solomon also had seventy thousand porters and eighty thousand quarrymen in the mountains, as well as the administrators' officials who supervised the work, three thousand three hundred of them in charge of the men employed in the work.

[6]

At the king's orders they quarried huge stones. . . .

This is an account of the forced labour King Solomon levied for the building of the Temple of Yahweh, his own palace, the Millo and the wall of Jerusalem, Hazor, Megiddo, Gezer, . . . Lower Beth-horon, Baalath, Tamar in the wilderness, inside the country, all the garrison towns owned by Solomon, all the towns for his chariots and horses, and all it pleased Solomon to build in Jerusalem, in Lebanon and in all the countries subject to him. [1 K 5:27-32; 9:15-19]

Later generations of Hebrews looked back to these times as the peak of their national glory, and their religious hopes centred on the restoration of the kingdom which David created and Solomon consolidated. The ancient kingdom of David and Solomon was an achievement whose effects can still be felt in our own times, for it is one of the main forces which have entered into the creation of the modern state of Israel. Yet it was only a minor, insignificant kingdom by secular historical standards, even in terms of the history of its own times; its brief achievements were only possible because of the temporary weakness of the great powers which surrounded it, and when those powers recovered their strength it was overwhelmed by them.

At the southern end of the coast road was Egypt. Egypt was the river Nile, and the river Nile was Egypt, so much so that the river gives a unity and continuity to an enormously wide range of history. In any other situation the history of Egypt would become the history of many different cultures and peoples. At the time of David and Solomon some of the pyramids were already nearly two thousand years old, and the great rock tombs

which became the fashion after the period of the pyramids were equally impressive memorials to the greatness
of their times. But the physical characteristics of the Nile
divided the people even while it gave them what unity
they possessed, for it created two distinct kinds of conditions for life. In Upper Egypt the river winds its narrow
way, without any tributary, through more than a thousand miles of desert, giving fertility to a narrow thread
of land on either side where the irrigation canals can
reach, and offering on its waters the only means of trans-
port and communication. The city of Thebes, a hundred
and fifty miles downstream from the first of the cataracts
which hinder navigation, was the main centre for this
long strip of civilisation, and when the power lay in
Upper Egypt it was the capital of the country. But as
the river nears the sea it runs into the great bulge which
it has pushed out into the Mediterranean, the delta
formed by the silt the river has carried with it, and here
its waters split into many channels which fan out over
an area two hundred miles long and a hundred miles
wide as the river finds its way to the sea. Here there
were a number of cities whose importance changed with
the political tide and with the shifting of the main river
channels: Tanis, Pi-Rameses, Pi-Beseth, Heliopolis,
which became capitals, or at least major royal residences,
when the people of the delta area were dominant.

During the time of Abraham and the Hebrew patri-
archs Egypt's influence had dominated the eastern coast
of the Mediterranean. For a hundred and fifty years from
about 1725 to 1575 BC, Egypt had been ruled by foreign
Asiatic kings, the Hyksos or 'Shepherd Kings', who set

[8]

up their capital at Avaris in the northeast part of the Nile delta. The native Egyptians of Upper Egypt were reluctant to accept this humiliation, despite an agreement which divided Egypt between the Theban rulers and the Hyksos at Avaris, and the Theban pharaoh Kamose started the war which his successors, Ah-mose I and Thut-mose I, carried to complete victory against the Hyksos. The way was open for establishing Theban rule again, more strongly than ever, throughout Palestine and Syria, and there is a vividly detailed description of the campaigns, including the capture of Megiddo, carved on the temple walls at Karnak. Despite the fears of his army commanders, Thut-mose III led his army through the narrow pass where the branch of the coast road climbs across the ridge of Mount Carmel; it took seven hours for the whole army to cover the six miles, but the defendants of Megiddo lost the opportunity presented to them, and the Egyptians took the city.

If the Egyptians had maintained their supremacy during the following centuries, the pattern of Hebrew history would have been very different, but a new pressure from outside, and internal troubles, forced the Egyptians to concentrate on the defence of Egypt itself without attempting to hold her foreign provinces. The main pressure seems to have been the result of the waves of migrations which swept in from the steppes of what is now Russia. People who were already settled were pushed further on, and some of them took to the sea. The pharaohs Merneptah and Ramesses III both repelled fierce attacks on Egypt by 'the peoples of the sea', and there is a full account of the fierce battle Ramesses III fought on the delta coast:

I have prepared the river mouths like a strong wall, with warships, galleys and coasters, fully equipped, for they were manned completely from bow to stern with valiant warriors carrying their weapons. The troops consisted of every picked man of Egypt. They were like lions roaring upon the mountain tops. The chariots consisted of runners, of picked men, of every good and capable chariot-warrior. The horses were quivering in every part of their bodies, prepared to crush the foreigners under their hoofs. I was the valiant God of War, standing fast at their head, so that they might gaze upon those whom my hands captured. . . . Those who came forward together on the sea, the full flame was in front of them at the river-mouths, while a stockade of lances confronted them on the shore. They were dragged in, enclosed, and prostrated on the beach, killed, and laid in heaps from tail to head. Their ships and their goods were as if fallen into the water. [Pritchard, *Ancient Near Eastern Texts,* 262f.]

The early years of the reign of Merneptah are the most attractive period for placing the exodus of the Hebrew slaves from Egypt and the journey round the Sinai peninsula and up the eastern side of the Dead Sea before entering Palestine opposite Jericho. Although Egypt repelled 'the peoples of the sea' she never recovered sufficient strength to assert her control over Palestine again, for the growth in power of the Theban priests led to civil war which left Egypt weakened beyond recovery of her former greatness. David and Solomon had the fortune to live during the declining period of this great civilisation.

At the other end the coast road ran across to the northern end of the basin of the rivers Tigris and

Euphrates, the second great cradle of civilisations in the Middle East. The Tigris and Euphrates both rise in the mountains of what is now Turkey, and in ancient times a network of irrigation canals connected to the two rivers made Mesopotamia famous for its agriculture. But, unlike Egypt, it was not easily defended. The long mountain chain which stretches from Turkey to the Indian Ocean harboured fiercely independent tribes, and the passes through the mountains permitted migrants to flood through from the eastern steppes beyond the Caspian Sea. The occupants of Mesopotamia had to be on constant guard, and it is not surprising that the history of the area is the rise and fall of power after power.

Somewhere about 1700 BC the Babylonian king Hammurabi conquered the Assyrians, destroyed Mari in the north, subjugated the ancient Sumerians, with their capital of Ur, in the south, and brought all of Mesopotamia under one rule. The prologue to the code of law which he promulgated and enforced sets out his achievements and the prosperity he brought to his people: reviving places which had declined, rebuilding ruins, and making irrigation and watering places to bring new areas under cultivation:

The ancient seed of royalty, the powerful king, sun of Babylon,
Who causes light to go forth over the lands of Sumer and Akkad;
The king who has made the four corners of the world subservient;
The favourite of Annani am I.

When Marduk commissioned me to guide the people aright,
To direct the land,
I established the law and justice in the language of the land,
Promoting the welfare of the people. . . .

[Pritchard, *Ancient Near Eastern Texts*, 165]

But for all his greatness, the prosperity Hammurabi created barely survived his death, for a wave of migrations
swept over Mesopotamia, and Babylon fell before it. Out
of the succeeding years of chaos a new Assyria arose and
for a brief span of a little over a hundred years the Assyrian power was supreme, but the slow pressure of the
migrating peoples, forced through the mountains by the
mass of moving tribes behind them, in turn forced the
Assyrians back, and although they retained control of
their homeland in the upper reaches of the Tigris round
Nineveh and Ashur, they no longer dominated Syria and
Palestine. Palestine was sealed off from Mesopotamia by
a Semitic people, the Aramaeans, emigrants who dominated the area north of Palestine at the same time as 'the
peoples of the sea' were trying to take over southern
Palestine and Egypt. The Aramaeans established small
independent states at Aleppo, Hamath, and Damascus,
and although they were none of them very strong, their
combined presence and their vague Semitic relationship
with the Hebrews was enough to protect Palestine from
Assyria.

The only serious threat to the Hebrews, as they infiltrated the Canaanites and by marriage or battle took
over the Jordan valley and the hills to the west of it,
came from the same 'peoples of the sea' who frightened
Egypt so badly. They settled on the coastal plain in a
loose federation of five cities, Gaza, Ashkelon, Ashdod,
Ekron, and Gath, and succeeded for a time in making

[12]

the Hebrews their subjects. As the Philistines they figure largely in the stories of Saul and David, but the very fact that so insignificant a people occupy so important a place in the biblical histories only shows how free the Hebrews were. If Egypt or Assyria had been able to spare time and energy to make their weight felt, neither the Philistines nor the Hebrews would have had any independence.

The complex balance of powers, and the geographical position of the Jordan valley, provided a small area of comparative calm for the Hebrews, so they could concentrate on the danger from the coastal plain to the west of them, where the Philistines had settled. East of the Jordan were the petty kindgoms of Edom, Moab, and Ammon, and then the impassable Syrian desert. The desert was formidable even to a people who used the recently domesticated camel, a territory where the most recent maps of our own times peter out into large blank areas with the word 'unsurveyed' printed across them.

The area of Palestine which the Hebrews were eventually to occupy was already settled by a people whose civilisation had once filled the whole area between Egypt and Mesopotamia. But conquest first by the Egyptians and then (at least along the coast) by 'the peoples of the sea', and pressure from successive waves of migration had weakened the Canaanites until they were in no position to offer effective resistance to the incoming Hebrews. In any case, their way of life was agricultural and city-centered, concentrated mainly in the fertile valleys, while the Hebrews were people with a nomadic tradition. At first, at least, the incoming Hebrew people would infiltrate into the hilly parts where they would find ample pasturage for their sheep and goats. In the very early stages they were not competing with the existing inhabitants for the agricultural areas (though that competition would quickly come), and their penetration lapped round the main Canaanite centres.

We have been left a vivid picture of life and conditions in Canaan, in the years before the Hebrews arrived, through the letters which have been discovered from local Canaanite kings to the Egyptian pharaohs. Egypt controlled the area at the time, and there was clearly an extensive correspondence involved in the administration and exploitation of Palestine. The country was divided between a number of small city-states, each with a central walled stronghold with its huddle of houses sheltering behind the fortifications. The foundation patterns of the parts that have been excavated show large differences between the sizes of the houses, clear indications that there was a wide range of social classes living within the cities. Each city controlled an area of cultivated land around it, but the people tending the land would return to the safety of the city at night, except perhaps during the intensive work of the harvests. Occasionally a city would have smaller fortified daughter cities under the rule of its king. Altogether the picture is not unlike Greece some six hundred years later.

Between the cities there was a constantly shifting pattern of enmity, alliance, suspicion, and distrust. Egypt's interest in the area was generated by its position on the only practicable route between Egypt and the north; for reasons both of defence and of trade she was concerned that there should be comparative peace there, and she installed officials and small, scattered garrisons of soldiers to guard her interests. In their turn, the local kings wrote to Egypt reporting, complaining, and asking for help. About a hundred and fifty years before the Hebrews arrived, the king of Megiddo wrote urgently to the Pharaoh Akhnaton, father of Tutankhamon:

Let the king know that ever since the archers returned to Egypt, Lab'ayu (king of Shechem) has carried on hostilities against me, and we are not able to pluck the wool, and we are not able to go outside the gate in the presence of Lab'ayu, since he learned that thou hast not given archers; and now his face is set to take Megiddo, but let the king protect his city, lest Lab'ayu seize it. Indeed, the city is destroyed from pestilence and disease. Let the king give one hundred garrison troops to guard the city. . . . [Pritchard, 485]

Lab'ayu was killed, as a later letter tells, and the siege raised, but the pettiness of the little war is shown by the request for such a small garrison force. Lab'ayu's two sons took up their father's cause and tried again to take Megiddo and make the people turn against Egypt. One sees why the people of Megiddo found it so necessary to dig a great tunnel connecting the centre of the city with the vital water spring at the foot of its walls.

Sometimes the threats came from the Egyptian soldiers sent as garrisons. Jerusalem had a small detachment of Egyptian army slaves stationed in the city who even went as far as looting the palace of the king of Jerusalem:

With reference to the Nubians, let my king ask the commissioners whether my house is not very strong! Yet they attempted a very great crime; they took their implements and breached the roof. If troops are sent into the land let them come with a regular Egyptian officer—for all the lands are impoverished by them—and let my king requisition for them much grain, much oil and much clothing, until the royal commissioner comes. . . . [Pritchard, 488]

The problem of who was to provide for the needs of troops stationed abroad was not just a modern one. The local Egyptian officials themselves were not above squeezing what they could out of the Canaanites; the king of Gezer, a little to the west of Jerusalem, wrote to the pharaoh asking for help against the Egyptian governor of Palestine:

Let the king, my lord, know the deed which Yanhamu did to me after I left the presence of the king, my lord. He seeks two thousand shekels of silver from my hand, saying to me: 'Give me thy wife and thy children, or I will smite!' Let the king know this deed, and let my lord send chariots to me, and let him take me to himself lest I perish! [Pritchard, 486]

There are even letters about an Egyptian governor who was in revolt against the pharaoh and had tried to turn the whole area against Egypt.

Migrant groups moving into the area from the semi-desert regions to the east were another source of trouble, and local kings appealed for troops to help resist their encroaches. These people are referred to as 'Apiru, and they may have been members of the same semi-nomad peoples to whom the Hebrews belonged. The

[16]

threat was sufficient to force the Canaanite kings, normally at war with each other, into alliances:

Let the king, my lord, learn that the chief of the 'Apiru has risen against the lands which the god of the king, my lord, gave me; but I smitten him . . . Zurata, king of Accho, and Indaruta, king of Achshaph, hastened with fifty chariots—for I had been robbed by the 'Apiru—to my help. . . . [Pritchard, 487]

It was Canaanite chariots, light horse-drawn vehicles of wood strengthened with iron, which struck such fear into the Hebrews when they met them in battle.

There are more peaceful glimpses in the letters of the trade which originated in the area, or passed through it on its way to Egypt. A copy of a letter from the Egyptian pharaoh to the king of Gezer lists the goods he is to collect ready for the Egyptian commissioner when he arrives:

Behold I am sending to thee Hanya, the commissioner of the archers, together with goods, in order to procure fine concubines, weaving women, silver, gold, linen garments, turquoise, precious stones, chairs of ebony, as well as every good thing, totalling 160 deben. Total: 40 concubines: the price of each concubine is 40 shekels of silver. So send very good concubines in whom there is no blemish. [Pritchard, 487]

It is more than probable that the king of Gezer was not above obtaining the goods for Egypt by robbing his fellow kings, for there is a letter from the king of Jerusalem complaining that he had sent off a caravan to Egypt with slaves, five thousand shekels of silver, and eight porters, but they were all captured while passing through the territory of the king of Gezer.

Shortly afterwards Egypt lost effective control of the area, mainly because of the arrival of 'the peoples of the sea', but there is no reason to think that the local life of the area changed so very much, for the new-comers remained largely in the coastal plains, until, as the Philistines, they tried to control the central highlands and the Jordan valley, and were defeated and confined by David. The Hebrews would find a people in posses-sion of the land who could have been formidable if they had been united amongst themselves, for their war techniques with 'iron' chariots and heavily fortified cities were far superior to anything the Hebrews had. It is possible also that the feudal social structure of the Canaanite cities, where the king virtually owned his land and people and ruled over a carefully stratified society, made for a more efficient army organisation than the Hebrews with their loosely organised tribes.

The city life of the Canaanites was to have a profound effect on the Hebrews, particularly after the consolida-tion of the nation's unity and the development of city life under David and Solomon, and the extent of the dangers of Canaanite influences on the Hebrews at the social level are vividly expressed by an anti-royalist account of the election of Saul to be first of the Hebrew kings. This particular version shows Samuel warning the people of the consequences of their request for a king, and it is clear that this reflects the character of Canaanite kingship:

'These will be the rights of the king who is to reign over you. He will take your sons and assign them to his chariotry and cavalry, and they will run in front of his chariot. He will use them as leaders of a thousand and leaders of fifty; he will make them plough his ploughland and harvest his harvest and make his weapons of war and the gear for his chariots. He will also take your daughters as perfumers, cooks and bakers. He will take the best of your fields, of your vineyards and olive groves and give them to his officials. He will tithe your crops and vineyards to provide for his eunuchs and his officials. He will take the best of your man-servants and maidservants, of your cattle and your donkeys, and make them work for him. He will tithe your flocks, and you yourself will become his slaves. When that day comes, you will cry out on account of the king you have chosen for yourselves. . . .' [1 Sm 8:11-18]

In view of the revolt which followed Solomon's reign, it is very probable that this situation was reached very quickly.

Yet the most profound dangers were to be found not in the social life of the Hebrews but in their religious life, and this danger was all the greater through the way in which the Hebrew people came to occupy the area. If their occupation had been a thoroughgoing and swift military conquest, as the book of Joshua presents it, they would have been more likely to reject everything Canaanite from the beginning. But it was not so. To a very large extent they mixed with the Canaanites, learned their techniques, and found their religion all too attractive:

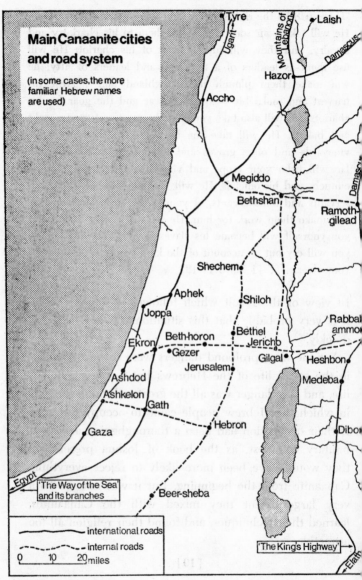

Main Canaanite cities and road system

(in some cases, the more familiar Hebrew names are used)

Tyre
Laish
Mountains of Lebanon
Damascus
Ugarit
Hazor
Accho
Megiddo
Damascus
Bethshan
Ramoth-gilead
Shechem
Shiloh
Aphek
Rabbah ammon
Joppa
Bethel
Ekron
Beth-horon
Jericho
Gezer
Gilgal
Heshbon
Jerusalem
Ashdod
Medeba
Ashkelon
Gath
Dibon
Gaza
Hebron
Egypt
'The Way of the Sea' and its branches
Beer-sheba

——————— international roads

- - - - - - - internal roads

0 10 20 miles

'The King's Highway'

Elath

The Israelites lived among the Canaanites and Hittites and Amorites, the Perizzites, Hivites and Jebusites; they married the daughters of these peoples, gave their own daughters in marriags to their sons, and served their gods. [Jg 3:5-6]

This seems a more likely account of the situation, for it is clear that there were important sections of the area, including Jerusalem and its district, which were still under Canaanite control until the time of David. The challenge of the native religions, and the assimilation of the religious experience which had produced them, was to be a most important factor in the development of the Hebrews' own faith as they explored the character of the God who had chosen them and brought them from Egypt to Canaan.

You might like to consider: what form changes in religious practices and statements of belief can take without betraying the truth which they claim to be preserving.

The People of the Covenant

A CCORDING TO the Pentateuch, it took forty years for the Hebrew tribes to travel from Egypt to Palestine, a distance of about four hundred miles even allowing for a route which went by way of the southern end of the Sinai peninsula; and of those forty years, thirty-eight were spent in the journey from Kadesh Barnea, at the southern end of Palestine, round to the Jordan valley opposite Jericho. The people could only move as fast as their grazing livestock would permit, but a more reasonable explanation for the length of time is to be found in the influences which affected the tradition about the journey. The section which gives this very long time for the journey reached the form in which we now have it during the exile in Babylon after the destruction of Jerusalem. Inevitably, that catastrophe was seen as punishment for the apostasy of the Hebrew people, and the length of the exile ensured that a whole generation would die out before there was any return and restoration of a purified people of God. So the people's reluctance to face the occupants of Canaan was seen as lack of faith in God, and they were condemned to wander in the desert areas at the foot of the Dead Sea until every doubting adult had died:

Then all the sons of Israel grumbled against Moses and Aaron, and the whole community said, 'Would that we had died . . . in this wilderness! Why does Yahweh bring us to this land, only to have us fall by the sword, and our wives and young children seized as booty? Should we not do better to go back to Egypt?' And they said to one another, 'Let us appoint a leader and go back to Egypt.'

Yahweh spoke to Moses and Aaron. . . .

'I have heard the complaints which the sons of Israel make against me. Say to them, "As I live—it is Yahweh who speaks— I will deal with you according to the very words you have used in my hearing. In this wilderness your dead bodies will fall, . . . all you who were numbered from the age of twenty years and over, you who have complained against me. I swear that you shall not enter the land where I swore most solemnly, to settle you. It is Caleb . . . and Joshua . . . [who withstood the complaints] and your young children that you said would be seized as booty, it is these I shall bring in to know the land you have disdained. As for you, your dead bodies will fall in this wilderness, and your sons will be nomads in the wilderness for forty years, bearing the weight of your faithfulness. . . ."'
[Nm 14:2-4; 26-33]

Such a comment makes sense in a situation where the nation's leaders were struggling to start again in Palestine after the exile in Babylon.

Two years is a more likely length of time for the

[24]

whole journey. Again, it is impossible to tell now whether the account of the repulse of the people in the area of Kadesh Barnea, as they tried to enter Palestine from the south, is probable; it may only be an echo of an earlier entry of related tribes through this area; but the main account takes the people up the Arabah, the deep continuation of the rift valley in which the Jordan and the Dead Sea lie, through the area east of the Dead Sea and across the Jordan opposite Jericho.

Whatever the length of time taken over the journey, it was sufficient to reestablish the structure and values of the tribes' traditional semi-nomadic way of life, and give it stability by grounding it firmly and thoroughly in the exodus experience. Whatever influences the people might be exposed to during the whole of the rest of their history, this wilderness journey remained the standard for their community life and for their relationships with God. It was the honeymoon period, of which the prophets were later to remind the people again and again when they were urging them to return to God:

That is why I am going to lure her
and lead her out into the wilderness
and speak to her heart.
I am going to give her back her vineyards,
and make the Valley of Achor a gateway of hope.
There she will respond to me as she did when she was young,
as she did when she came out of the land of Egypt.

[Ho 2:16-17]

In the most remarkable way, however much the external circumstances of their lives changed as they came under

[25]

the influence of other cultures, this remained the norm by which everything they assimilated was tested.

It is by no means certain that all of the tribes entered Palestine at the same time, nor, even, that all of them had been in Egypt. The letters from the Canaanite kings to Egypt show that infiltration of nomadic groups from the semi-desert areas was a constant problem, and clearly this is part of the same pattern of movement which T. E. Lawrence found still operating amongst the Arab tribes fifty years ago and which he called 'the circulation which kept vigour in the Semitic body'. It was formed by the attraction of permanent pasturage and dependable crops, and the pressure from the nomadic peoples which forced the weaker peasant groups off their land and out into the desert to become nomads in their turn: 'There were few, if indeed there was a single northern Semite, whose ancestors had not at some dark age passed through the desert. The mark of nomadism, that most deep and biting social discipline, was on each of them in his degree.' [1] Against this background the vital factor is not that the tribes should all have entered Palestine at the same time, nor even that they should all have shared in the exodus experience; it lies in their recognition that they had things in common which distinguished them sharply from the Canaanites: the belief that they were related to each other by a common ancestry, the semi-nomadic life which had left such a deep mark on their social institutions and their personal relations, and the worship of Yahweh. An examination of the groups of Hebrew people involved in the events of the

[1] T. E. Lawrence, *Seven Pillars of Wisdom*, chapter 2.

Book of Judges suggests, in fact, that only the northern group was involved in the exodus experience and the entry into Palestine across the Jordan after the journey through the wilderness. It seems probable that the people of Judah and Simeon were already settled in the south, separated from the northern group by the central group of Canaanite cities, including Jerusalem. But they would have sufficient in common with the northern tribes to accept their experience as their own, and the new understanding of the power and love of their God Yahweh as a fact which they also wished to share.

The basic pattern of Hebrew life took its shape from the needs of comparatively small groups of people whose lives depended on carefully organised movement to ensure that their flocks were adequately fed. The extended family forming a clan was the natural unit, under the direction of the most senior, capable man in the clan, and all the institutions arose from this basic family pattern. There was a real and fundamental equality between the members of the family; disputes were settled by the head of the clan, solely, so far as we know, in the light of the consequences of this equality and without the kind of complex, formal legal code based on the authority of royal decree. One of the few fragments of legal code that can be dated with confidence from the times before the entry into Palestine, the 'lex talionis'—an eye for an eye and a tooth for a tooth— is based fundamentally on this equality, limiting revenge or punishment to the extent of the original injury. This fundamental basis of Hebrew law was retained even after the original society had been radically changed by the rise of a permanent monarchy, and there is a vivid example of it in practice in the famous confrontation of David by the prophet Nathan. Nathan put 'a case' to David, and at the end of it David gave judgement without hesitation:

David's anger flared up against the man. 'As Yahweh lives,' he said to Nathan, 'the man who did this deserves to die! He must make fourfold restitution for the lamb, for doing such a thing and showing no compassion.' [2 Sm 12:5-6]

In any other civilisation throughout the history of the Near East, from Hammurabi right through to Roman times, the king would first have had to enquire about the status of the man who had committed the offence: whether he was a noble, a freeman or a slave. The laws of the 'sabbatical year' and the 'Jubilee year', when debts were written off and slaves were given their freedom if they wanted it, were intended to guard this equality, however much they might have been ignored in practice. Equality only applied to members of the Hebrew tribes, of course, and the law recognised the enslavement of peoples who were not entitled to be members of the central assembly of the tribes.

This approach to fellow members of the community was sharply contrasted with the Canaanite social system, where the king of a city and its district was the sole owner of the land; citizens could only use land by a feudal relationship with the king, and even when a system of wider land ownership developed in the Canaanite cities the strict social divisions and legal distinctions remained. The strength with which the Hebrews defended the right of the individual to own

land is well illustrated by the incident of Naboth's vineyard three hundred and fifty years after the entry into
Palestine. Ahab, king of the northern kingdom, Israel,
wanted a piece of land to extend his palace gardens and
was refused by the owner:

Ahab said to Naboth, 'Give me your vineyard to be my
vegetable garden, since it adjoins my house; I will give you
a better vineyard for it or, if you prefer, I will give you its
worth in money.' But Naboth answered Ahab, 'Yahweh forbid
that I should give you the inheritance of my ancestors!'
[1 K 21:2-3]

Ahab's wife Jezebel had Naboth murdered so that her
husband could obtain his land, and Elijah prophesied
the end of Ahab's dynasty as a punishment for the
crime. This guarding of the rights of the individual to
his land, and its roots in the family, is also shown by the
law which gave other members of the family the first
option if land was put up for sale, and the purchase of
poor men's land by the rich was one of the evils
repeatedly condemned by the prophets, for the practice
eroded one of the main foundations of equality and
independence in the society.

After the Hebrews took to city life, the law continued
to be administered by the heads of the families living
in the city, the 'elders at the gate', in direct continuation
of the practice of the nomadic tribe. The only legal
authority above these local 'lay magistrates' (who, it is
to be noticed, were not *appointed* by anyone—they
merely exercised a natural right arising directly from
their status as head of a family)—the only superior

authority—was the solitary 'judge' whose successive names are listed in Judges 10:1-5 and 12:7-15. These are to be distinguished from the 'major' judges of the period, military leaders who arose to deal with a particular military crisis. The 'minor' judges have no military function. There is no information about how they were chosen, and their function was probably connected with the divine law of the convenant, the law which concerned the people as a whole, rather than the local law of the individual communities. That local law was administered in the most public place possible, the open space immediately inside the city gate, and the guarantee of its fairness and consistency was that its administration was witnessed by any of the citizens who cared to watch. One of the new developments which emerged with the monarchy was the practice of taking cases to the king to be heard, and the appointment of deputies by the king to administer justice:

whenever a man with some lawsuit had to come before the king's court, Absalom would call out to him and ask, 'What town are you from?' He would answer, 'Your servant is from one of the tribes in Israel.' Then Absalom would say, 'Look, your case is sound and just, but there is not one deputy of the king's who will listen to you.' [2 Sm 15:2-3]

This was one of the points where the new monarchy radically modified the life of the local Hebrew communities.

So far, these people might have been any of T. E. Lawrence's semi-nomadic Semitic groups moving in from the desert and gradually becoming settled peasants who squeezed out or absorbed the people already in possession of the land. One single factor singled them out and distinguished them from all other groups: their religious experience.

Their worship was centred on the kind of act one would naturally expect from a shepherd community: the sacrifice of a lamb. Moreover, the circumstances of the sacrifice met the needs of a group which was regularly on the move as the sparse pasturage in any one area was eaten. The lamb was sacrificed with everyone packed and ready to move; no utensils were needed, except, perhaps, a basin to catch the blood; it was eaten with unleavened bread and wild herbs; and whatever remained uneaten at the end of the sacrifice was burned so that the site could be left clear of remains. It is not clear whether this sacrifice was only an annual one, possibly at the time of the spring lambing, or whether it was part of the ritual for moving camp at any time. The latter is the most likely, for part of the ceremony consisted of smearing the blood of the victim on the tent posts. This was because it was thought that the life of an animal was to be found in its blood, and this sanctified life would be a powerful protection against any evil they might meet during the vulnerable moving period. There was no priesthood involved, for the head of the family naturally presided over the sacrifice, and this remained a characteristic of the Passover throughout Hebrew history—yet another reminder of the original undifferentiated society on which their lives were based.

The central physical symbol of their religion was a portable shrine, the Ark, which was the outward sign of the presence of God in their midst. The descriptions of the construction of the Ark in the Book of Exodus are quite late, but they may be taken as an elaboration of a continuing tradition; it is depicted as a wooden chest, three feet nine inches long and two feet three inches in each of the other dimensions, with pairs of rings for carrying-shafts, and the whole chest covered and lined with gold. On the chest, and covering the whole of the top, was the gold 'throne of mercy' and at each end of the throne there was a golden cherub with wings spreading out over the throne. The throne was for God:

There I shall come to meet you; there, from above the throne of mercy, from between the two cherubs that are on the ark of the Testimony, I shall give you all my commands for the sons of Israel. [Ex 25:22]

Inside the Ark were two stone tablets with the Decalogue carved on them. An earlier section of the tradition gives ritual formulae to be said in association with the Ark's movements, and these point clearly to the belief that it was the place of God's presence:

And as the ark set out, Moses would say,
'Arise, Yahweh, may your enemies be scattered
and those who hate you run
for their lives before you!'
And as it came to rest, he would say,
'Come back, Yahweh,
to the thronging hosts of Israel.' [Nm 10:35-36]

The tradition that the Ark contained copies of the basic law to which the people as a whole were subject may be

[32]

later, but the close association of law with the presence of God is at the heart of the matter.

All this could be no more than the religious practices of any nomadic Semitic group, but for one thing. The people related it all to their experience during the exodus from Egypt. Against all odds, and beyond anything that could have been achieved by human ability alone, they had escaped from forced labour in Egypt and had seen a detachment of the Egyptian army, with its dreaded chariots, bog down as it pursued them through the marshes at the northern end of the Red Sea and the soldiers drown when the wind dropped and the water flowed back again. Somewhere in the course of their subsequent journey the whole group had experienced the confirmation of this as the proof that their God, Yahweh, was present amongst them and had chosen them and demonstrated his power to them. Whatever their beliefs about Yahweh had been before, it could now be summed up in the words of Jethro, Moses' father-in-law, when he met the people in the desert and heard of their escape:

'Blessed be Yahweh' . . . 'who has rescued you from the Egyptians and from Pharaoh, and has rescued the people from the grasp of the Egyptians. Now I know that Yahweh is greater than all the gods . . .' [Ex 18:10-11]

Their God had entered into a covenant with them; he had proved his power and his protection of them, and in turn he required that their behaviour should reflect the new relationship which he had established with them. Unlike every other people of their time the law which expressed that relationship was primarily concerned with the way in which the people were to treat each other, and only secondarily concerned with the details of their worship and sacrifices. However much the Ten Commandments may have been expanded and modified before they reached the form in which we now have them (and there is no evidence to suggest that they have suffered much modification), their basic pattern is authentic: the first four are concerned with exclusive loyalty to Yahweh, and the remaining six specify this loyalty in terms of the kind of personal relations which must be found amongst these people whom Yahweh had chosen and made his own.

It is this close relationship between a law of personal behaviour and the worship of their God which more than anything else marked the difference between the Hebrew people and the Canaanites. For the Canaanites' religion was essentially a fertility cult serving their agricultural needs, and the religious practices involved struck at the roots of personal relationships. However much the Hebrews—and their kings—might be attracted by it, and even think it was an essential part of the new agricultural techniques they learned from the Canaanites, in the end the memory of the exodus, and of the character of their God who had revealed himself to them, would force them to reject the Canaanite religion and try to stamp out all traces of it. The excavation of the site of the ancient city of Ugarit at Ras Shamra on the Syrian coast of the Mediterranean brought to light a large collection of religious texts; these gave detailed information about the Canaanite religion at the time the Hebrews arrived in Palestine. The complex myths are woven round a pantheon of gods who control the agricultural year; the growth and decay of the crops reflected the annual conflict between gods representing life and death, and the fertility of both animals and the land depended on the sexual intercourse of the gods. The pantheon ranged from gods whose powers were thought to extend throughout the world, to local Baals and Asherahs (male and female) whose influence was confined to a small district or even to a field. The cult associated with this worship involved sacral prostitution and the reenacting of the myths; the Adonis cult belonged to this area too.

Two factors made the Canaanite religion a dangerous influence on the incoming Hebrews. The first, and lesser, danger arose from the adoption by the Hebrews of various Canaanite shrines as their central sanctuary. The Hebrew tribes formed a loosely organised confederation, the focus of which was the Ark. This was set up first at Shechem, then moved to Bethel, Gilgal, and finally to Shiloh. At Shiloh it fell into Philistine hands and then reached its final permanent resting-place when David took it to Jerusalem. Shechem, Bethel, Gilgal, and Shiloh were all ancient Canaanite religious shrines, but this does not mean that the Hebrews took over Canaanite cultic practices when they used one of their sacred sites. A site could not be 'made' sacred by human activity, it had to become sacred through some manifestation of divine power in connection with it, and it was understandable that the Hebrews would use places which the local people already associated with the supernatural.

All the accounts agree that a central feature of Hebrew worship around the Ark was the reading and reaffirmation of the divine law during a ceremony of renewal of the covenant with Yahweh. Joshua 24 gives a detailed description of such a ceremony; after recounting the events of the exodus and the entry into Palestine, the people declared their exclusive loyalty to Yahweh, and Joshua recorded the event:

That day, Joshua made a covenant for the people; he laid down a statute and ordinance for them at Shechem. Joshua wrote these words in the Book of the Law of God. Then he took a great stone and set it up there, under the oak in the sanctuary of Yahweh, and Joshua said to all the people, 'See! This stone shall be a witness against us because it has heard all the words that Yahweh has spoken to us: it shall be a witness against you in case you deny your God.' [Jos 24:25-27]

The Hebrews could only use such a site with the consent of the local Canaanite community, and it is possible that the movements of the Ark to different sites reflect the people's changing relations with various Canaanite cities; but the Ark was, after all, a portable shrine and its movements may have been no more than a continuation of the traditions associated with it.

The more serious danger from Canaanite religion arose as the Hebrews learnt the techniques of Canaanite agriculture, for those techniques were closely bound up with the Canaanite religion. The process of separating the two was difficult and was still a major problem right up to the Babylonian exile over six hundred years later. All of the major prophets had to wrestle with the task of weaning the people away from the fertility cults, and the drastic measure of limiting all sacrifice solely to the temple in Jerusalem, which Josiah tried to enforce in 622 B.C., shows how real the problem was. Hosea's denunciations, delivered to the northern kingdom just after 750 B.C., are typical:

a prostituting spirit leads them astray,
they renounce their God to play the whore.
They offer sacrifice on the mountain tops,
burn their offerings on the hills,
under oak and poplar and terebinth,
so pleasant is their shade.
So, although your daughters prostitute themselves
and your sons' wives commit adultery,
I shall not be hard on your daughters for their whoring
or on your sons' wives for their adultery,
when everyone else is wandering off with whores
and offering sacrifices with sacred prostitutes.
Thus does a senseless people run to ruin.

[Ho 4:12-14]

The solution had to lie in the realisation that it was their own God, Yahweh, who was the source of all fertility and life:

She would not acknowledge, not she,
that I was the one who was giving her
the corn, the wine, the oil,
and who freely gave her that silver and gold
of which they have made Baals.

[Ho 2:10]

[37]

This realisation was part of the long growth towards monotheism; the seeds of it had been planted at the exodus, when the escape was seen as Yahweh's victory over the Egyptian gods, but the full application of it to the details of everyday life took a very long time.

An important step in the rejection of the Canaanite religion came through the use made of the Canaanite harvest festivals. There were three main harvest festivals in the year, corresponding with the three main crops. The first, in March or April, was for the barley harvest, the second was seven weeks later at the end of the wheat harvest, and the last was in September or October when the autumn gathering of grapes and garden fruits took place. The Hebrews eventually tied all these harvest festivals to their own Passover sacrifice, and so associated them all with the exodus experience. They were helped in this by the date and character of the first of the harvest festivals; it occurred at the same time as the Hebrews celebrated the Passover, and one of its principal features, from which it took its name, was that the people only ate unleavened bread during the eight days of the feast. This was probably because the yeast was thought to profane the purity of the dough, and the first part of the harvest was particularly holy to the god who had produced it. Unleavened bread was part of the Hebrew Passover rite also. The Feast of Unleavened Bread was attached to the Passover by the simple act of celebrating the Passover the day before the Feast of Unleavened Bread started. Once this attachment had been made the association of the other feasts of the year followed, and the whole agricultural year could become a further expression of the power of the same Yahweh who had brought them out of Egypt. By the time of the Deuteronomic Code, the main part of which probably reached its present form about 650 BC, the process was complete, and may have been for some time before that:

'You are to count seven weeks, counting these seven weeks from the time you begin to put your sickle into the standing corn. You must then celebrate the feast of weeks for Yahweh your God. . . . You must rejoice in the presence of Yahweh your God. . . . Remember that you were a slave in Egypt, and carefully observe these laws.' [Dt 16:9-12]

In the end, the victory of Yahweh over the Canaanite gods, in an area which so vitally affected the people's everyday lives, is a testimony to the strength and reality of the exodus experience which the Hebrews brought with them into Palestine.

You might like to consider: by what means, and through what channels, religious faith should be brought to bear on the secular life of a society.

The Judges

W HEN THEY reflected on the history of their nation, later Hebrew historians saw the disasters as punishment for apostasy, and the obvious apostasy, which cried out on every hilltop sanctuary and in every little figurine of the mother goddess, was the Canaanite fertility cult which touched the people's lives so closely. The power of Yahweh, so impressively demonstrated at the exodus, had to be effective in every detail of daily life, and this could not be while the peasant digging in his field or the mother nursing her child looked for security to Baal or Astarte. The historical books in the Bible were not written for academical interest; they had an urgent pastoral function to perform amongst the people who listened to them read, and this pastoral concern shows in every word. Little wonder, then, that the historians put into Moses' mouth the kind of language they were sure he would have used if he had been living in their own times. It was their way of bringing the

covenant experience to bear on their own times to provide the solution to the intensely urgent problems they
saw around them in the people's lives:

'When Yahweh your God has led you into the land you are
entering to make your own, many nations will fall before
you: Hittites, Girgashites, Amorites, Canaanites, Perizzites,
Hivites and Jebusites, seven nations greater and stronger
than yourselves. Yahweh your God will deliver them over to
you and you will conquer them. You must lay them under
ban. You must make no covenant with them nor show
them any pity. You must not marry with them: you must
not give a daughter of yours to a son of theirs, nor take a
daughter of theirs for a son of yours, for this would turn
away your son from following me to serving other gods and
the anger of Yahweh would blaze out against you and soon
destroy you. Instead, deal with them like this: tear down their
altars, smash their standing-stones, cut down their sacred poles
and set fire to their idols. For you are a people consecrated to
Yahweh your God; it is you that Yahweh our God has chosen
to be his very own people out of all the peoples on the earth.'
[Dt 7:1-6]

No doubt the people teaching this point of view would
point out that both Isaac and Jacob had gone to great
lengths to find brides from amongst their own kinsfolk.

This deuteronomic viewpoint has strongly influenced
the account of the occupation of the Promised Land,
both in the selection of the material and the way in
which it is presented. This is particularly true of the
Book of Joshua, but it is clearly evident in the Book of
Judges as well. Each of the tribes would have had its

own local traditions in which it preserved the memories of how it acquired the territory it occupied; although the account in Joshua seems at first sight to deal with the whole country, a closer examination shows that it is mainly concerned with the territory occupied by the tribe of Benjamin. The Benjamin traditions must have fitted the historian's purposes well, for they dealt with the area where the Israelites from Egypt crossed into Palestine, and the mountainous region which Benjamin took over had only a few scattered Canaanite settlements which were quickly overcome. Jericho, on the western edge of the Jordan valley, was the only place of any size, but despite the extensive excavations that have been carried out on the site it is still not clear whether it was fully occupied and fortified when the Hebrews came to it. We have to bear in mind all the time that the historians were living in the experience of the horrors of Manasseh's reign, the failure of Josiah's great attempt at drastic reform, and the destruction of Jerusalem by the Babylonians.

Fortunately there is sufficient scattered material for us to get some idea of how the occupation of the land proceeded, at any rate, in the northern parts. Clearly, the Israelites first moved into the areas which were only thinly occupied by the Canaanites, the high ground which was unsuitable for agriculture. Even here there is enough evidence to show that the picture was by no means always one of conquest and destruction, for the Canaanite city of Shechem appears as one of the clans which formed the tribe of Manasseh, and in the conventional way of showing who were true Israelites Shechem is named as a 'son' of Manasseh (Nm 26:31). In Joshua there is a whole section to account for the acceptance of four Canaanite cities in the heart of the Benjamin territory itself (Jos 9); though here the Canaanites are made to accept an inferior status. The position was reversed further north. The tribe of Issachar moved into the highly fertile valley of Jezreel, dominated by Megiddo, and they were tolerated by the Canaanites provided they were prepared to accept a position of subservience:

'Issachar is a strong ass,
lying down in the midst of the sheepfolds.
He saw how good it was to take his ease,
how pleasant was the country,
so he bowed his shoulders for the load,
he became a slave to forced labour.' [Gn 49:14-15]

There is an interesting passage in one of the Amarna letters which shows that this was a normal situation in the Jezreel area, and although the letter belongs to a slightly earlier period than the arrival of Issachar, it helps to authenticate the picture:

Let the pharaoh be informed concerning his servant (the king of Megiddo) and concerning his city. Behold, I am working in the town of Shunama, and I bring men for forced labour, but behold, the governors who are with me do not work in the town of Shunama, and they do not bring men for forced labour, but I alone bring men for forced labour. . . . [Pritchard, 485]

Zebulun and Asher, in the region north of Jezreel, may have had to accept some form of feudal service supplying the shipping trade of the Phoenician coastal towns in exchange for being allowed to occupy the land.

In one case, the tribe of Dan, they settled west of Benjamin's territory where the central highlands run down to the coastal plain, and were then pushed out by the 'peoples of the sea' as they arrived from across the Mediterranean and began to push inland. Of the seventeen towns named as belonging to Dan in the lists in Joshua, the twelve that have been identified all lie in the plains southeast of Joppa, and one of them, Ekron, became a Philistine city. The people of Dan moved to the far north above the Sea of Galilee, captured Laish and changed its name to Dan:

men of the tribe of Dan set out from Zorah and Eshtaol, six hundred of them, armed for war. They went up and camped at Kiriath-jearim in Judah . . . [and] From there they entered the highlands of Ephraim and came to Micah's house. [Jg 18:11-13]

There they persuaded a Levite priest to leave Micah and become the priest for the tribe, bringing with him the sacred image from Micah's household shrine:

So taking with them the god that Micah had made and the priest who had served him, the Danites marched against Laish, against a peaceful and trusting people. They slaughtered all the inhabitants and set the town on fire. There was no one to help the town because it was a long way from Sidon and had no relations with the Aramaeans. . . . They rebuilt the town and settled in it, and called it Dan after Dan their father. . . . The Danites erected the carved image for their own use. [Jg 18:27-30]

There are many points of interest in the story, for it points to the emergence of a professional priesthood held by members of the tribe of Levi; it shows how a tribe attached importance to its own local sanctuary with its sacred image, alongside its loyalty to the central sanctuary of the confederation, and it enables us to relate the arrival of the Philistines, the 'peoples of the sea', to the settlement period of the Israelites.

Two significant facts emerge as we look at the overall picture of the settlement. Firstly, Jerusalem and the area around it remained in Canaanite hands, and to the west of Jerusalem the area is quickly reached where the Danites were repulsed by the Philistines as they grew in strength. It looks as if there was a belt of territory right across the country separating the north from the south, and the story of the Levite who travelled with his concubine from Bethlehem, south of Jerusalem, to the Benjamin territory in the north, suggests that it was an area of danger:

By the time they were near Jerusalem, the day was fast going. The servant said to his master, 'Please let us leave the road now and enter this Jebusite town and spend the night there.' His master answered, 'We will not enter a town of foreigners, of people who are not Israelites; we will go on to Gibeah [in Benjamin] instead.' He went on to say to the servant, 'Come on, we will try to reach one or other of those places, either Gibeah or Ramah, and spend the night there.' [Jg 19:11-13]

Secondly, with the single exception of a brief passage early in Judges, the southern tribe of Judah, with which

Simeon is also associated, plays no part in the events of the Book of Judges. All the action lies with the northern tribes, and it is at least possible that Judah took no part in the settlement events described in Joshua and Judges, and that they were not amongst the tribes who came from Egypt. If this is so, it is a powerful testimony to the strength of the exodus experience that the southern tribes should also identify themselves with it. Their kinship with the tribes who had taken part in the covenant, and the evidence of longstanding Yahweh worship in the Judah area, would be sufficient for them to consider that the covenant applied to them as well. All told, the separation of the northern and southern groups of tribes, and the difficulty of movement between the two areas, goes a long way towards explaining how easily the nation split into two kingdoms after the death of Solomon.

Very little is known about the normal organisation of the Israelites as a whole during the years before Saul became the first king. They were held together by their share in the covenant experience and their loyalty to the central sanctuary, wherever the Ark happened to be at any time, and there may have been a permanent official concerned with law, the 'minor judges' already mentioned in the previous chapter: Tola, Jair, Ibzan, Elon, and Abdon. They all came from places in the northern part of the country. The narrative in Judges is concerned with the times of disturbance and danger, when a leader emerged to cope with the particular crisis. His authority was essentially charismatic: 'And

[47]

the spirit of Yahweh came on Gideon. . . . The spirit of Yahweh came on Jephthah. . . . The spirit of Yahweh seized on him, and though he had no weapon in his hand he tore the lion in pieces as a man tears a kid . . .' (Jg 6:34; 11:29; 14:6; etc.), and he is called a judge only in the sense of restoring the peace of the covenant. If in fact he continued to rule so that 'the land enjoyed rest' after the crisis was over, this was a direct result of the proof he had given in battle that he really did possess the spirit of God.

The incidents described, and the judges who emerged to deal with them, show the range of dangers the Israelites had to face during this period of settlement. The first, Othniel, is too vague for us even to be certain about the danger he faced. As the text stands (Jg 3:7-11), he repelled an attack from a Mesopotamian king, or a Syrian one, but it may be better to read 'Edom' instead of 'Aram' in the text (in the Hebrew the difference would only mean substituting a *daleth* for a *resh*, and the two letters are very similar in shape) and see it as an attack against the Judah tribes from the little kingdom at the foot of the Dead Sea. Othniel is associated with people who belonged to the south, so this lends support to this view, though the evidence is altogether too scrappy for certainty.

The second judge, Ehud, arose during a period when the king of Moab, the kingdom east of the Dead Sea, had succeeded in conquering the tribe of Benjamin and forced them to pay tribute money. Ehud saved the situation by being left-handed, and the story is in the best tradition of single-handed adventures:

[48]

Ehud made a dagger—it was double-edged and a cubit long—
and strapped it on under his clothes, over his right thigh. He
presented the tribute to Eglon the king of Moab. This Eglon
was a very fat man. Having presented the tribute, Ehud
went off again with the men who had carried it; but he
himself, on reaching the Idols of Gilgal, turned and went
back and said, 'I have a secret message for you, O king.' The
king replied, 'Silence!' and all who were with him went out.
Then Ehud went in. The king sat in the cool retreat of his
upper room; he was alone. Ehud said to him, 'I have a message from God for you, O king.' The king immediately stood
up from his seat. Then Ehud, using his left hand, drew the
dagger he was carrying on his right thigh and thrust it into
the king's belly. The hilt too went in after the blade, and the
fat closed over the blade, for Ehud left the dagger in his
belly; then he went out through the window. [Jg 3:16-22]

He then rallied the Israelites at the Jordan fords and cut
the Moabites down as they tried to return to their own
country.

Leaving Shamgar aside, for the solitary verse (Jg
3:31) which mentions him belongs properly after the
Samson cycle at the end of Judges 16, the next major
incident occurred eighty years after Ehud when
Deborah, a prophetess, with the aid of Barak as chief of
staff, defeated a coalition of Canaanite cities in the
valley of Jezreel (Jg 4-5). The Canaanite army broke
before the Israelite charge, despite their chariots, and
here the Israelite use of Mount Tabor may have enabled
them to force the battle to take place where the ground
was unfavorable to chariots. It is significant that the
Canaanite commander, Sisera, fled on foot, and was
murdered by a Kenite woman who offered him shelter.

This campaign is the first mention of united military action by a group of Israelite tribes, including tribes such as Issachar which had been living in a state of near slavery to the Canaanites, so we may conclude that by this time the Israelites had gained the ascendancy over the Canaanite cities in the north, for there is no further mention of danger from Canaanites.

Issachar itself provided the next judge, forty years later, when Gideon defeated attacks from nomadic groups who came in from the eastern desert. This is a fascinating situation, for we may see in it the effects of the domestication of the camel which was achieved about this time; it enabled the nomadic desert peoples to swoop into the fertile agricultural areas, raid the crops and return safely to the desert oases again:

Whenever Israel sowed seed, Midian would march up with Amalek and the sons of the East; they would march up against Israel and encamp on their territory and destroy the produce of the country as far as Gaza. They left Israel nothing to live on, not a sheep or ox or donkey, for they came up as thick as locusts with their own cattle and their tents; they and their camels were past counting, they overran and pillaged the country. [Jg 6:3-5]

Gideon captured a Midianite camp and followed it up with a campaign into the eastern desert regions where he took the retreating main group of nomads by surprise. He then completed the operation by subduing the Israelite cities on the eastern side of the Jordan, which, naturally enough, had refused to cooperate with the campaign; they lay on the main routes the nomads took as they came in from the desert, and while the main body remained undefeated they evidently thought their best course was to remain neutral (Jg 6-8). At Gideon's death there is the first hint of a government more permanent than the charismatic leader, and the extension of a single partiarchal rule over several tribes. One of Gideon's sons, Abimelech (which means 'father of the king'), murdered his brothers and was proclaimed king by a group of Israelites at Shechem, but his reign ended in revolt and he was killed while trying to defeat the rebels.

The list of neighbouring eastern states to threaten the Israelites is completed with the attack by the Ammonites, a kingdom to the east of Jordan around the region of Amman, the modern capital of the Arab kingdom of Jordan (Jg 10:6-12). The leader who arose in this situation was Jephthah, who belonged to the Israelite region of Gilead, just east of Jordan and bordering on the Ammonites. Jephthah defeated the Ammonites, but the main interest in the story centres in Jephthah's sacrifice of his daughter:

And Jephthah made a vow to Yahweh, 'If you deliver the Ammonites into my hands, then the first person to meet me from the door of my house when I return in triumph from fighting the Ammonites shall belong to Yahweh, and I will offer him up as a holocaust.' . . .

As Jephthah returned to his house at Mizpah [after victory], his daughter came out from it to meet him; she was dancing to the sound of timbrels. This was his only child; apart from her he had neither son nor daughter. When he saw her, he tore his clothes and exclaimed, 'Oh my daughter,

[51]

what sorrow you are bringing me! . . . I have given a promise to Yahweh, and I cannot unsay what I have said.' She answered him, 'My father, you have given a promise to Yahweh; treat me as the vow you took binds you to. . . . Grant me one request. Let me be free for two months. I shall go and wander in the mountains, and with my companions bewail my virginity.' . . . When the two months were over, she returned to her father, and he treated her as the vow that he had uttered bound him. [Jg 11:30-39]

It cannot be doubted that the editor of these stories, at the least, believed that human sacrifice was still a possibility amongst the Israelites at this time, and we may see darker connections still with the Tammuz cult of Mesopotamia in which women wept for Tammuz in the course of the annual fertility cycle. The understanding of the implications of the covenant still had a very long way to go.

With the Samson stories (Jg 13-16) the Book of Judges arrives at the first serious mention of the Philistines, and from now onwards they dominate the scene until their decisive defeat at the hands of David about 1000 BC. For a hundred and fifty years they controlled the region, and the geographical name, Palestine, maintains the memory of their power. No Philistine documents have been discovered, so we are dependent on the Bible, and the Egyptian accounts of the battles against the 'peoples of the sea', for all our information about them. So used are we to thinking of them from the Hebrew point of view that it comes as a surprise to think of the situation as the Philistines must have seen it: 'They established themselves in strongholds from which they resisted the assaults of the Hebrews. The resistance of the Philistines was so stubborn that the land of Canaan subsequently became known as Palestine.'[1] Philistine soldiers are shown in Egyptian carvings wearing tufted headdresses and short kilts, and they settled on the coastal plain in five cities: Gaza, Ashkelon, and Ashdod along the coastal road, and Gath and Ekron further inland. They were organised in a loose confederation in which each city had a king, and in times of war they elected one of the kings as commander-in-chief for the duration of the campaign. Although they were not Semites, from the evidence of the names of their gods (and so far there has been nothing else to work from), they adopted the Canaanite religion. Their arrival in Canaan somewhere about 1200 BC marks the end of the Bronze Age in the region, for they brought with them the secret of working in iron. It is difficult to be sure how far this gave them an advantage in weapons; in the Egyptian carvings they are shown armed with circular shields and swords, and Goliath carried a bronze javelin and iron-tipped spear in addition to his sword, and the sword was almost certainly an iron weapon. During the period of Philistine control of the Israelites they carefully controlled the use of iron:

There was not a single smith in the whole land of Israel, because the Philistines had reasoned: We must prevent the Hebrews from forging swords or spears. Hence all the Israelites were in the habit of going down to the Philistines

[1] Jean Delorme in *Larousse Encyclopedia of Ancient & Medieval History*, London 1963, 79.

THE COVENANT AND THE KINGDOM

to sharpen every ploughshare, axe, mattock or goad. [1 Sm 13:19-20]

Iron had entered into the construction of Canaanite chariots, but its use must have been very restricted for there to be so little knowledge of how to work it.

Looked at from the military point of view, Samson's exploits against the Philistines are only spasmodic and ineffective, and there is no trace of any organised campaign or rallying of the tribes; he was just a local strong man whose exploits have passed into legend. The remaining judge, Shamgar, who should be placed at the time of Samson, was equally ineffective, it seems, so far as any lasting results are concerned. All that Judges says about him is that 'He routed six hundred of the Philistines with an ox-goad; he too was a deliverer of Israel' (Jg 3:31). Clearly, the Philistines were rapidly gaining control of the region.

They made that control complete in a battle fought about 1050 BC on the coastal plain near Aphek, about ten miles inland from the modern Tel Aviv. There is no mention of the name of the Israelite commander, for this was a decisive defeat, and in any case the focus of the action was not a military leader, it was the sacred Ark of the covenant. The battle developed in two engagements:

The Philistines drew up their battle line against Israel, the battle was hotly engaged, and Israel was defeated by the Philistines and about four thousand of their army were killed on the field. [1 Sm 4:2]

The defeated army extricated itself and returned to camp, there the elders of Israel decided to fetch the Ark from the central sanctuary at Shiloh and carry it into battle. They could be sure, then, that God really would be with them, and defeat would be impossible. They were wrong; whatever the power of God that was focused round the Ark, it was not to be used in that way:

So the troops sent to Shiloh and brought away the ark of Yahweh Sabaoth, he who is seated on the cherubs. . . . When the ark of Yahweh arrived in the camp, all Israel gave a great shout so that the earth resounded. When the Philistines heard the noise of the shouting, they said, 'What can this great shouting in the Hebrew camp mean?' And they realised that the ark of Yahweh had come into the camp. . . . 'Alas!' they cried, 'This has never happened before. Alas! Who will save us from the power of this mighty God? It was he who struck down Egypt with every kind of plague! But take courage and be men, Philistines, or you will become slaves to the Hebrews as they have been slaves to you. Be men and fight.' So the Philistines joined battle and Israel was defeated, each man fleeing to his tent. The slaughter was great indeed, and there fell of the Israelites thirty thousand foot soldiers. The ark of God was captured too. . . . [1 Sm 4:4-11]

The sacred Ark, the symbol of Israelite unity and of the power of God present and active amongst them, was in Philistine hands; although the Philistines found it an embarrassing possession, their capture of it was an effective sign of their complete victory. They kept it for seven months, but so many frightening things happened in its vicinity that they sent it out of their homeland back towards Israelite territory. There it came to rest at Kiriath-jearim on the borders of Benjamin and Judah, and there it stayed for fifty years until David had captured Jerusalem and could move it to his new capital.

The Philistines moved in to control the Israelite territory and established a permanent garrison, possibly with a resident governor, in the heart of the Benjamin country at Gibeah. The stage was set for the rise of the monarchy in Israel, for it was at Gibeah that Saul, the first king, was born.

You might like to consider: whether we too can or should see a religious meaning in our history.

Saul

IT IS LITTLE wonder that the books of the Bible which deal with the reigns of Saul and David are called the Books of Samuel, for at a superficial reading the first one is dominated by the prophet Samuel, and the critical moment in David's reign came when he had to choose whether he would rule as God's viceroy or be a typical Canaanite king whose actions were only controlled by the limitations of his actual political power. Samuel had warned the people that their desire for a king was a rejection of God's rule. The whole subsequent history of the monarchy can be read in the light of that warning.

In fact, when the text of the Books of Samuel is examined more closely it is easy to see that a number of traditions have been woven very loosely together without much attempt to reconcile the divergencies of viewpoint. The main blocks of material used seem to have been two traditions of the life of Samuel, two traditions of the way in which David entered the service of Saul, stories about David's childhood, a history of the struggle for the succession which went on throughout the later years of David's reign, lists of officials and outstanding men in David's reign, and a block of material about the movements of the sacred Ark. We are moving now into the period when regular records were kept in written form, so the men who assembled and edited the accounts of this period would have more tangible material to work with than the oral traditions about earlier times; fortunately, they stitched the different patches of material together in pieces, instead of weaving it afresh into a single homogeneous unity which only expressed one point of view, so it is fairly easy to separate the different strands.

The sharp differences noticeable are the result of two very different attitudes towards the monarchy. One of them, the earlier, was sympathetic towards being ruled by kings, and we may see here, perhaps, the hand of a group of court officials during the reigns of David and Solomon and a little later; but the other, later attitude is strongly critical of the effects of kingly rule on the lives and religion of the people. One effect of this is a heightening of the authority and achievements of Samuel until he is depicted as a king in all but title and a prophet of the stature and wide influence of an Isaiah or a Jeremiah. It is easy to see how this came about. Even after the division of the nation into two rival kingdoms at the death of Solomon, the rule of the early kings was centred on the worship of Yahweh although other cults were tolerated. But from 721 BC the position changed radically. The northern kingdom, Israel, was destroyed by the Assyrians at the request of their southern brethren in the kingdom of Judah, and the Judaean king, Ahaz, introduced the Assyrian cult into the centre of the worship in the temple in Jerusalem as part of the price for Assyrian help:

When King Ahaz went to Damascus to meet Tiglath-pileser king of Assyria, he saw the altar that was in Damascus [Assyria had just captured Damascus]. He then sent the measurements and a model of the altar with the detail of its workmanship to Uriah the priest. Uriah the priest constructed the altar. . . . When the king arrived from Damascus, he inspected the altar, he approached it and ascended it. He burned his holocaust and his oblation; he poured out his libation and sprinkled the blood of his communion sacrifice. The altar that used to stand before Yahweh he removed from the front of the Temple. . . . King Ahaz gave this order to Uriah the priest: 'In future you will burn the morning holocaust, the evening oblation, the king's holocaust and his oblation, the holocaust, the oblation and the libations of all the people on the great altar; on it you will pour out all the blood of the holocausts and sacrifices. . . . 'Uriah the priest did everything that King Ahaz had ordered. [2 K 16:10-16]

His successor, Hezekiah, managed to reform matters for a while, but the rot had truly set in; his son Manasseh led the people into the depths of degradation in the course of his fifty-year reign. Once more the rot was stopped by the deuteronomic reform of King Josiah, but again the work was undone by the four kings who reigned in the twenty years that remained before the Babylonians destroyed Jerusalem. It is not surprising that the men who lived through these experiences looked at kings with cautious eyes and dreamed of keeping them under the careful control of prophets and priests.

So the story of Samuel starts with the dedication of the child to the service of God at the central sanctuary at Shiloh. There he was put in the charge of the sanctuary priest, Eli, and very soon found himself called to denounce Eli for allowing his sons to run riot; the child Samuel began his task of keeping the people faithful to the covenant:

Yahweh then came and stood by, calling as he had done before, 'Samuel! Samuel!' Samuel answered, 'Speak, Yahweh, your servant is listening.' Then Yahweh said to Samuel, 'I am about to do such a thing in Israel as will make the ears of all who hear it ring. On that day I will carry out against Eli everything I have spoken about his House, from beginning to end. You are to tell him that I condemn his House for ever because he has known that his sons have been cursing God, yet he has not corrected them. Therefore—I swear it to the House of Eli—neither sacrifice nor offering shall ever expiate the guilt of the House of Eli.' [1 Sm 3:10-14]

Soon, all the people knew that there was a prophet in the land, and the capture of the sacred Ark by the Philistines, with the death of Eli's sons in the battle and of Eli when he heard the news, confirmed Samuel's position.

So runs the anti-royalist account, and 1 Samuel 7-8 and 12 give us a picture of the adult Samuel defeating the Philistines and ruling all the northern section of the country, travelling in circuit to hear the more difficult legal cases and to preside at the sacrifices at the main shrines. There need never have been any question of a king, it seems, but for the unworthiness of Samuel's sons:

But his sons did not follow his ways; they wanted money, taking bribes and perverting justice. Then all the elders of Israel gathered together and came to Samuel at Ramah. 'Look,' they said to him, 'you are old and your sons do not follow your ways. So give us a king to rule over us, like the other nations.' . . . Yahweh said to Samuel, 'Obey the voice of the people in all that they say to you, for it is not you they have rejected; they have rejected me from ruling over them. All they have done to me from the day I brought them out of Egypt until now—they deserted me and served other gods—they are doing now to you. Well, then, obey their voice; only, you must warn them solemnly and instruct them in the rights of the king who is to reign over them.' [1 Sm 8:3-9]

So Samuel duly gave way to the people, warned them of the foolishness of their request: 'You will cry out on account of the king you have chosen for yourselves, but on that day God will not answer you' (1 Sm 8:18), and then himself chose Saul by casting the sacred lots amongst all the tribes of Israel. Samuel's exit from the scene occupies the whole of 1 Samuel 12; it has all the flavour of the bitter old man of the family who has suddenly discovered that the children have grown up.

But there is another point of view, another strand of tradition, and on the face of it this one is a more likely account of the situation in the middle of the eleventh century BC when Saul rose to power. For it is consistent with the picture we have of the Israelite community in

[61]

the Book of Judges, and it sets Saul's rise firmly within the context of national need. That need was again felt by a small Israelite community, Jabesh-Gilead, on the eastern slopes of the Jordan valley, where a valley drains down from Ammonite territory. The people had a walled city to retreat to, but an Ammonite raiding party besieged it until the people had to plead for terms. The Ammonite terms were harsh: submission and the acceptance of mutilation; the people of Jabesh were given seven days to decide. Messengers from Jabesh appealed for help from the Benjaminites, their neighbours across the Jordan, and Saul, son of one of the elders of Benjamin, took charge of the situation:

Saul was just then coming in from the fields behind his oxen, and he said, 'What is wrong? Why are the people weeping?' They explained to him what the men of Jabesh had said. And the spirit of Yahweh seized on Saul when he heard these words, and his fury was stirred to fierce flame. He took a yoke of oxen and cut them in pieces which he sent by messengers throughout the territory of Israel with these words: 'If anyone will not march with Saul, this shall be done with his oxen!' At this, a dread of Yahweh fell on the people and they marched out as one man. [1 Sm 11:5-7]

The Ammonite besiegers were routed, and Saul's position was as certain as that of any of the judges before him who had won their right to rule through victory in battle.

It was a small, local engagement, but it filled the people with the hope that they could turn towards a larger victory: the expulsion of the Philistines who had

conquered and garrisoned the land. They had found a
leader who had proved that he had the spirit of God;
his authority would be even more effective if they made
him their king. The defeat of the Ammonites is told
within the context of the account of the coronation of
Saul, and it is not easy at this remove to tell what the
sequence of events was. As it stands, Saul was anointed
king by Samuel a month before the Ammonite battle,
but the anointing was kept secret until the people proclaimed Saul king at the sanctuary at Gilgal after his
success. What is significant is the picture of Samuel in
this account, for he is clearly no more than the local
religious figure, a man with a reputation for possessing
second sight, who was at most the guardian of the tribe
of Benjamin. Nevertheless, he would be the natural person to turn to when Saul the Benjaminite was to be
made king, for the central act involved pouring consecrated oil on the head of the king-elect. It was a ceremony which the Israelites probably copied from the
surrounding kingdoms, for the olive was the most common fruit tree and the oil pressed from the olives entered
deeply into the everyday lives of the people; it figured
largely in their cooking, provided the fuel for the lamps,
and was used for personal hygiene. It was also used
ritually in a number of ways, including the emancipation
of slaves and the purification of cured lepers. It is easy
to see how it came to be associated with the possession
of strength, and when it was consecrated and poured on
a man it gave him divine strength, 'the spirit of God';
once this sacred anointing was performed the man was
set apart for life, and any man who harmed him committed sacrilege.

[63]

It was a radically new development in the life of the Israelite community, for so far all authority had been exercised by the community as a whole, except in times of immediate danger, and even though the charismatic leader continued to stand out in the community after the danger had passed, the people as a whole regained their corporate power each time the situation settled down again. Now power had been institutionalised in a central authority, and the tension between the community and the government which was to last through the rest of Israelite history had begun. Potentially, it was a radical change in the nature of the society which had been created by the covenant experience. There is a strong hint of this tension even in the sympathetic account of Saul's election as king: 'But there were some scoundrels who said, "How can this fellow save us?" They despised him, and offered him no present' (1 Sm 10:27).

But whatever the tension latent in the new institution, the situation forced it into the background, for Saul immediately took the initiative, while the people were still assembled for his coronation, and started a revolt against the Philistines by attacking the garrison posts in his home territory:

Jonathan smashed the Philistine pillar which was at Gibeah and the Philistines learned that the Hebrews had risen in revolt. Saul had the trumpet sounded throughout the country, and the whole of Israel heard the news: Saul has smashed the Philistine pillar, and now Israel has incurred the enmity of the Philistines. So all the people rallied behind Saul at Gilgal. [1 Sm 13:3-4]

The Philistines reacted swiftly, marched a large force into the heart of the Benjamin territory at Michmash, where it was protected to the front by a deep valley, and set up strongholds from which they could dominate all the northern part of the area. Here Jonathan, Saul's son, took the initiative again, and with his armour-bearer crept up on the Philistines and succeeded in driving in one of the outposts of the main camp:

There was panic in the camp and in the countryside; all the men in the outpost, and the raiding contingent too, were terrified; the earth shook; it was a very panic of God. Saul's lookout men in Geba of Benjamin could see the camp scattering in all directions.

Saul then said to Ahijah, 'Bring the ephod' [to consult God]. . . . But while Saul was speaking to the priest, the turmoil in the Philistine camp grew worse and worse; and Saul said to the priest, 'Withdraw your hand.' Then Saul and the whole force with him formed up and advanced to where the fighting was, where men were all drawing their swords on each other in wild confusion. The Hebrews who had earlier taken service with the Philistines and had accompanied them into camp, themselves defected to the Israelites with Saul and Jonathan. All the Israelites in hiding in the highlands of Ephraim, hearing that the Philistines were on the run, chased after them and joined in the fight. That day Yahweh gave Israel the victory, and the battle spread beyond Beth-horon. [1 Sm 14:15-23]

The first decisive blow against the Philistines had been struck, yet all through the accounts there runs the tension between the sacred and the secular, the men of God and the civilian political power, a tension exposed and aggravated by the new instrument of government.

At the opening of the revolt against the Philistines the later account describes a scene between Saul and Samuel, for Saul had waited seven days for Samuel to come and offer the sacrifices for the army, and had then offered them himself. Inevitably, Samuel arrived in the middle of the ceremonies, accused Saul of disobedience, and prophesied his rejection by God. There is an anachronism here, of course, for at this period it was still normal for the army commander to preside over sacrifices before battle and it is hard to see where Saul was at fault, but even the earlier account shows Saul moving into battle, in the height of the emergency created by Jonathan's attack on the Philistine outpost, without first consulting the sacred lots.

But the tension shows itself most clearly in the sacred war against the Amalekites. After Saul's successful revolt the Philistines withdrew to their coastal territory; they had no permanent central government for their federation and they supplemented their army with mercenaries, so it would take them a little time to appoint a national commander and organise a force strong enough to reconquer the Israelites. During the lull Saul made sure that the frontiers to the east and north were secure and then turned his attention to a tribe of nomads in the south, the Amalekites. We can see at this moment the first clear signs of an Israelite state with recognisable frontiers, and the end of the period of occupation by infiltration, consent, and local conquest. Saul turned his attention from the needs of defence and consolidation to national revenge. During the march through the Sinai peninsula the Israelites had been opposed by the Amalekite tribe of nomads, understandably, for they were moving through Amalekite territory and using the pasturage on which the Amalekites depended in their cycle of nomadic movement. Saul moved against the Amalekites in what may be the first example of the nation acting as a whole to uphold the honour of their covenant with God. There is a hint in 1 Samuel 14:48 that the Amalekites had been raiding the Israelites settled in the southern parts of Palestine, but in the whole of the following chapter there is no suggestion of any territorial reason for the campaign. They had opposed the people of God; God must be avenged. The expedition was successful, but the religious purpose of it required the destruction of the Amalekites and all their property, and here Saul held his hand:

Saul then defeated the Amalekites, starting from Havilah in the direction of Shur, which is to the east of Egypt. He took Agag king of the Amalekites alive and, executing the ban, put all the people to the sword. But Saul and the army spared Agag with the best of the sheep and cattle, the fatlings and lambs and all that was good. They did not want to put those under the ban; they only put under the ban what was poor and worthless. [1 Sm 15:7-9]

Samuel arrived on the scene, and despite Saul's pleas that they had only saved the best animals for sacrifices to God, denounced Saul for disobedience:

Then Saul said to Samuel, 'I have sinned, for I have transgressed the order of Yahweh and your directions, being afraid of the people and doing what they said. Now, I pray you, forgive my sin; come back with me and I will worship

Yahweh.' But Samuel answered Saul, 'I will not come back with you, for you have rejected the word of Yahweh and he has rejected you as king of Israel.' As Samuel turned to go away, Saul caught at the hem of his garment and it tore, and Samuel said to him, 'Today Yahweh has torn the kingdom of Israel from you and given it to a neighbour of yours who is better than you.' . . . 'I have sinned,' Saul said, 'but please still show me respect in front of the elders of my people and in front of Israel, and come back with me, so that I can worship Yahweh your God.' Samuel followed Saul back and Saul worshipped Yahweh. [1 Sm 15:24-31]

Samuel then killed Agag himself. This is clearly the later view, with its inflation of Samuel, its distrust of kings, and its concern that there should be no compromise with anything that threatened the purity of the covenant. Saul in fact continued to rule, and under his rule there was a further victory over the Philistines, but in the end he failed, and failed in the very thing which had brought him to power: battle against the nation's enemies. This is the real proof for his contemporaries that God had withdrawn his favour from him, and it is only natural that they should see this final failure already at work in earlier events in his reign. One single factor reconciles the contradictions: no matter what he might do, he had been anointed, and this sacred character and responsibility must not be opposed by any merely human power. Moreover, he was still the king whom the northern group of Israelites had chosen, and there is no hint yet that their loyalty to him had diminished. He still held the political power, despite Samuel's denunciations.

Saul not only failed in the end; the shadows in his character and his reign are also deepened by contrast with the king who followed him. That king was David, the standard by which all subsequent kings were assessed and the root from which the ideal of the Messiah grew when faith in earthly kings died. It is not surprising that traditions arose around him; more surprising, perhaps, is the remarkably human and credible picture of him which emerges from the fifty-nine chapters of the Bible devoted to him. In view of his achievements and the place he occupied in the nation's history, the way in which he became a member of Saul's court and rose to power was particularly important. It had to be emphasised that there had been no usurpation of authority, no opposition to Saul, God's anointed, and this theme runs right through the chapters describing David's relationship with Saul and continues into the accounts of the critical early years of David's reign. It was equally important to show that Saul had welcomed David and personally appointed him to a position of military responsibility; and one may even see the proof of David's right to reign in his defeat of Goliath, just as the charismatic leaders before him had shown that they had the spirit of God when they were victorious in battle. When these factors are borne in mind it is easy to see why the text contains blatant contradictions. The compiler had before him accounts written for different purposes and in differing situations, and the text shows it.

So the story of David opens with Samuel choosing him by lot from amongst his brothers and anointing him secretly, then he entered Saul's service as an armour-bearer and a musician with the skill to soothe Saul during spells of melancholy. But David's real rise from obscurity came when the Philistines returned in force. At this point there is no sign that Saul or anyone at his court had ever heard of David, and he only became involved when his father sent him to the Israelite camp with food for his brothers serving with the army. There he found that the Philistines had sent forward a champion with a challenge to single combat and had found no Israelite willing to accept it. There was no question of the single combat deciding the issue between the Philistines and the Israelites, but whichever man won would certainly strengthen the morale of the army to which he belonged. David offered his services to Saul, refused the handicap of armour, and advanced on the Philistine with his shepherd's weapon of a sling and stones:

He took his staff in his hand, picked five smooth stones from the river bed, put them in his shepherd's bag, in his pouch, and with his sling in his hand he went to meet the Philistine. The Philistine, his shield-bearer in front of him, came nearer and nearer to David; and the Philistine looked at David, and what he saw filled him with scorn, because David was only a youth, a boy of fresh complexion and pleasant bearing. The Philistine said to him, 'Am I a dog for you to come against me with sticks?' And the Philistine cursed David by his gods. . . .

No sooner had the Philistine army started forward to confront David than David left the line of battle and ran to meet the Philistine. Putting his hand in his bag, he took out a stone and slung it and struck the Philistine on the forehead; the stone penetrated his forehead and he fell on his face to the ground. Thus David triumphed over the Philistine with a sling and a stone and struck the Philistine down and killed him. David had no sword in his hand. Then David ran and, standing over the Philistine, seized his sword and drew it from the scabbard, and with this he killed him, cutting off his head. [1 Sm 17:40-51]

The Israelite army attacked and the Philistines were routed.

Immediately after the battle and pursuit Saul called David to him, asked him who he was, and commanded him to join the court; there, David's position was secured by friendship with Saul's son Jonathan, and he was given command of the royal bodyguard:

Saul kept him by him from that day forward and would not let him go back to his father's house. Jonathan made a pact with David to love him as his own soul; he took off the cloak he was wearing and gave it to David, and his armour too, even his sword, his bow and his belt. Whenever David went out, on whatever mission Saul sent him, he was successful, and Saul put him in command of the fighting men; he stood well in the people's eyes and in the eyes of Saul's officers too. [1 Sm 18:2-5]

David had arrived, welcomed by the man whose failure would make his own success even more striking. The narrative could move on safely to the first indications of the enmity with Saul which was to drive David from court and, at one stage, to service with the Philistines as a mercenary.

The tension began, where one would expect, when David gained a greater reputation than Saul as a soldier.

His military reputation was the foundation of Saul's power, yet the songs in the streets were unfavourably contrasting Saul's reputation with David's:

On their way back, as David was returning after killing the Philistine, the women came out to meet King Saul from all the towns of Israel, singing and dancing to the sound of tambourine and lyre and cries of joy; and as they danced the women sang:

'Saul has killed his thousands,
And David his tens of thousands.'

Saul was very angry; the incident was not to his liking. 'They have given David the tens of thousands,' he said 'but me only the thousands; he has all but the kingship now.' And Saul turned a jealous eye on David from that day forward. [1 Sm 18:6-9]

The song sounds authentic and certainly travelled far, for a Philistine officer quoted it later to support his reluctance to have David marching with them as they moved against Israel for the battle in which Saul was killed. An uneasy period at court began, eased only by the friendship of Jonathan, who at one stage brought about a reconciliation by pleading to his father for David. Saul gave David one of his daughters, Michal, in marriage, but only after he had promised him his eldest daughter, Mereb, and then given her to another man; even the betrothal of Michal was made to depend on David performing a dangerous military feat in which Saul hoped he would be killed, but David successfully obtained two hundred Philistine foreskins instead of the mere hundred Saul had asked for.

[72]

The final breach came through a further military success by David against the Philistines. Saul could not control his jealousy and tried to kill David with his own hand. He fled to his house and when Michal warned him that Saul had posted agents to murder him as he left in the morning, he escaped by a window and fled. Even now he hoped that he might be able to return to the court, so Jonathan arranged a signal so that he could safely tell David whether he could return. But Saul was implacable. David's absence confirmed Saul's suspicions of treason, and Jonathan's excuses for him only caused further anger:

Jonathan answered Saul, 'David asked urgent leave of me to go to Bethlehem. "Please let me go," he said, "for we are holding the clan sacrifice in the town and my brothers have ordered me to attend. So now if you approve of this, let me take my leave and see my brothers." That is why he has not come to the king's table.'

Then Saul's anger flared up against Jonathan and he said to him, 'You son of a wanton! Do I not know that you are in league with the son of Jesse to your own disgrace and the disgrace of your mother's nakedness? As long as the son of Jesse lives on the earth neither your person nor your royal rights are secure. Now, send and bring him to me; he is condemned to death.' [1 Sm 20:29-31]

Next morning Jonathan went out with a servant to a place where David could see him from his hiding-place, shot an arrow and shouted to his servant the words which he and David had arranged as a warning: 'Is not the arrow ahead of you? Be quick, hurry, do not stand about!' The final scene between David and Jonathan,

[73]

which follows immediately, is certainly the result of some storyteller's sense of climax, for if it could have occurred there would have been no need for the secret signal. David fled into exile.

You might like to consider: whether the church has a prophetic duty, at international, national, and local levels, to intervene in politics; and, if it has such a duty, what form this intervention should take.

The Young David

THE LAST years of Saul's reign are set in the framework of Saul's hatred of David, and of the tightrope walked by David to keep his life intact and at the same time avoid doing anything which would be remembered against him when he came to the throne. David the warrior is still there, even to the extent that he and the men who followed him lived by the sword, but David the extremely able politician becomes more and more conspicuous. He was helped by the conditions of his times. The kingdom bore little resemblance to anything we would recognise by that name; for one thing, Saul's rule was only effective in the north, and even there it is doubtful whether he had much influence far from Benjaminite territory. Jerusalem was still in Canaanite hands and the Hebrews living in the south were at best only loosely associated with the northern confederation. If, as is quite likely, these southern Hebrews had not entered the country at the same time as their northern brethren, Saul's rule over them would be very uncertain. David was himself a southerner, from Bethlehem, four miles south of Jerusalem, and could count on a certain amount of southern support and sympathy when he fled from Saul. Saul's rule was further limited by the Philistines. They only accepted their defeats as temporary setbacks, and they still controlled a great deal of the south, so much so that Saul's pursuit of David into the south must have been a risky undertaking. Furthermore, wandering bands of armed men seem to have been a common feature, for there is evidence that such bands hired themselves as mercenaries in time of war and lived at other times by charging 'protection' to the districts through which they moved in times of peace. The presence of the Philistines was the really serious factor in the situation, and on the face of it David appears to have played a very dangerous game with them.

David's first act was to make for the sanctuary at Nob, close to Jerusalem, where the priest of the sanctuary, Ahimelech, gave him food and Goliath's sword. For several reasons this was an important sanctuary; Goliath's weapons were stored there as trophies of God's victory, through David, over the Philistines. Moreover, Ahimelech was the descendant of Eli, the guardian of the sacred Ark when it was taken by the Philistines and its sanctuary at Shiloh destroyed. If we are to look for a national sanctuary during this interim period Nob would be the place, and it is certain that David was looking for more than food and weapons—he would also want reassurance that he was not acting against God's will by his flight. One of Saul's servants, Doeg, was also there, and reported to Saul that the priests had helped David. The results were disastrous for the priests:

Doeg the Edomite then spoke up . . . 'I saw the son of Jesse come to Nob to Ahimelech, . . . son of Ahitub. This man consulted Yahweh for him, gave him provisions and also the sword of Goliath the Philistine.' Then the king sent and summoned the priest Ahimelech son of Ahitub and his whole family, the priest of Nob; they all came to the king. . . .

The king said to the guardsmen who were standing beside him, 'Step forward and put the priests of Yahweh to death, for they too have supported David, they knew he was making his escape yet did not tell me.' But the king's servants would not lift a hand to strike the priests of Yahweh. The king then said to Doeg, 'You step forward and strike the priests.' Doeg the Edomite stepped forward and struck the priests himself, that day killing eighty-five men who wore the linen ephod. As for Nob, the town of the priests, Saul put it to the sword, men and women, children and infants, cattle and donkeys and sheep.

One son only of Ahimelech . . . escaped. His name was Abiathar, and he fled away to join David. . . . [1 Sm 22:9-20]

David had begun to gather around him the men who were to become the chief officers of his kingdom.

The early stages of David's flight are full of confusion. His first move was to seek refuge at Gath, the most inland of the five Philistine towns, but although he had broken with Saul his reputation in the skirmishes with the Philistines told against him and he only escaped by pretending to be mad. He then settled for a while in a group of caves on the western slopes of the Judaean highlands. There he was joined by his parents and

[77]

family, and by a number of people with various private reasons for fleeing from society: 'All the oppressed, those in distress, all those in debt, anyone who had a grievance, gathered round him and he became their leader. There were about four hundred men with him' (1 Sm 22:2). It was an outlaw group, in fact, and it is not surprising that Saul should attempt to stamp it out. David realised there was bound to be trouble for such a collection, and he took his parents to safety in Moab, on the eastern side of the Dead Sea.

The need to move from the caves near Adullam came quickly when David led his small force to protect the people of Keilah, just south of Adullam, against a Philistine raiding party. The Philistines were robbing the people of their harvest, laid out on the town's threshing floors, no doubt a common experience for the people who lived on the edge of the Philistine territory. The Philistine party must have been small and unimportant, for their defeat did not prevent the Philistines from giving David refuge shortly afterwards, but it gave Saul the information he needed for finding David, and raised in him the hope that he could trap him in a walled town. Caught between the Philistines, Saul and David, the villagers would certainly have handed David over, so he and his followers fled into the wild country at the southern end of the Judaean hills, where the ground falls away to the Dead Sea, four thousand feet below. Even here it was necessary to keep on the move, for there are incidents which belong to various places from the wilderness of Ziph, just south of the ancient southern sanctuary of Hebron, down to Engedi on the shores of the Dead Sea. It is a desolate, forsaken area, remote and inaccessible, ideal for men fleeing from authority. Ten miles south of Engedi, and a thousand years later, 967 people held out for three years at Masada against a Roman legion, before committing suicide to avoid surrender.

The problem of feeding the group was solved by David in a time-honoured way. He exacted 'protection' money from the shepherds in the hills:

When David learned in the wilderness that Nabal was at his sheepshearing, he sent ten soldiers, saying to them, 'Go up to Carmel [the Judaean village, not the northern range], visit Nabal and greet him in my name. You are to say this to my brother, "Peace to you, peace to your House, peace to all that is yours! I hear that you have the shearers; now your shepherds were with us and we did not molest them, nor did they find anything missing all the time they were at Carmel. Ask your soldiers and they will tell you. May these soldiers win your favour, for we come on a day of feasting. Whatever you have to hand please give to your servants and to David your son." ' [1 Sm 25:4-8]

Foolishly, Nabal refused, and David set off towards him with a force of four hundred men. If Nabal's wife, Abigail, had not heard and hurriedly set off for David secretly with a mass of provisions, Nabal would have himself been shown how important it was to pay for David's kindness. As it was, the news that his wife had bought David off was too much for him:

Abigail returned to Nabal. He was holding a feast, a princely feast, in his house; Nabal was in high spirits, and as he was very drunk she told him nothing at all till it was daylight. In the morning then, when the wine had left him, his wife told him all that had happened and his heart died inside him and he became like a stone. About ten days later Yahweh struck Nabal, and he died.

When David heard that Nabal was dead, he said, 'Blessed be Yahweh who has avenged the insult I received at Nabal's hands and has restrained his servant from doing evil; Yahweh has brought Nabal's wickedness down on his own head.' [1 Sm 25:36-39]

It comes as no surprise that David then married Abigail, 'a woman of intelligence and beauty'. He was already married to Ahinoam, from the Judaean village of Jezreel. His marriage to Saul's daughter, Michal, was temporarily in abeyance, as Saul had given her to one of his Benjaminites.

During this period there occurred an incident which is of great importance for the light it throws on David's attitude towards the authority of the king, an attitude which he would want others to have when he in turn became king. There are two accounts of the incident, in 1 Samuel 24 and 26, and it may well be that the accounts are of two similar situations, but they are so similar that it is more reasonable to think that they are two versions of the same event. Saul pursued David into the remote parts where he was hiding, for he was far too serious a threat to the throne to leave free if he could be captured or killed. During the hunt, Saul unsuspectingly camped near the place where David and his men were hiding, and David was able to get near enough to kill him:

David went to the place where Saul had pitched camp. He saw the place where Saul and Abner son of Ner commander of his army were lying. Saul was lying inside the camp with the troops bivouacking round him. . . .

David said, 'Who will come down with me into the camp of Saul?' Abishai answered, 'I will go down with you.' So in the dark David and Abishai made their way towards the force, where they found Saul lying asleep inside the camp, his spear stuck in the ground beside his head, with Abner and the troops lying round him.

Then Abishai said to David, 'Today God has put your enemy in your power; so now let me pin him to the ground with his own spear. Just one stroke! I will not need to strike him twice.' David answered Abishai, 'Do not kill him, for who can lift his hand against Yahweh's anointed and be without guilt? As Yahweh lives,' David said, 'Yahweh himself will strike him down, whether his time to die comes, or he goes out to battle and perishes then. Yahweh forbid that I should raise my hand against Yahweh's anointed! . . .' [1 Sm 26: 5-11]

So they took the spear, and a pitcher of water, and stole away again. When they were at a safe distance David taunted Saul's bodyguard with his feat, and asked Saul for reconciliation. The account makes Saul penitent for all that he had done to David, and it even ends with Saul saying, 'May you be blessed, my son David! You will do great things and will succeed' [1 Sm 26:25], but David's actions give no support for this, for he decided that the chase was becoming too hot for him, and with his six hundred followers he moved down to Gath and offered his services to the local Philistine king.

He was welcomed, and was paid for his service by being given the city of Ziklag, deep in the south of Judah. There he and his force guarded the district against the incursions of the tribes of the southern desert, and convinced the Philistines that they were maintaining the Philistine rule over the Judaeans as well. It was a delicate situation, for his future rule was to depend on Judaean support in its early stages, but not as delicate as the situation which was developing between the Philistines and Saul.

The final reckoning for Saul was approaching as the Philistines again gathered their strength and set up a central organisation to march against him in force. Saul mobilised the Israelite forces, and then found that he could obtain no indications of success from Yahweh: 'Saul consulted Yahweh, but Yahweh gave him no answer, either by dream or oracle or prophet' (1 Sm 28:6). In his anxiety he turned to the necromancers, the spiritualist cult of the dead which he had himself forbidden. Disguised, and with only two of his followers, so as not to awaken suspicion, he travelled up to Endor in the valley of Jezreel, and there he consulted a woman whom his followers had said could bring up the spirits of the dead. It is a strange scene, and deeply moving: the frightened and disguised king meeting the woman in the night, and the woman afraid that it is all a trap:

But Saul swore to her by Yahweh, 'As Yahweh lives,' he said, 'no blame shall attach to you for this business.' Then the woman asked, 'Whom shall I conjure up for you?' He replied, 'Conjure up Samuel.'

Then the woman saw Samuel and, giving a great cry, she said to Saul, 'Why have you deceived me? You are Saul.' The King said, 'Do not be afraid! What do you see?' The woman answered Saul, 'I see a ghost rising up from the earth.' 'What is he like?' he asked. She answered, 'It is an old man coming up; he is wrapped in a cloak.' Then Saul knew it was Samuel and he bowed down his face to the ground and did homage. [1 Sm 28:10-14]

But there was no comfort for him. Samuel could only predict disaster:

Tomorrow you and your sons will be with me; and Israel's army, too, for Yahweh will deliver it into the power of the Philistines. [1 Sm 28:19]

Moved by the sight of the distraught king, who still had her life in his hands, the woman comforted Saul, prepared food for him and persuaded him to eat. After he had eaten, he returned to his army and the battle of Gilboa.

Meanwhile, the Philistines had concentrated at Aphek, the northernmost town in their home territory, and David had had to contribute his force to the Philistine army which Achish of Gath marched to join. But his reputation saved him from having to fight against Saul. There is evidence that the word 'Hebrew' may have been a general term for a mercenary band at this time, so the question the other Philistine leaders asked Achish was a natural one: 'Who are these Hebrews?'

Achish replied . . . , 'Why, this is David the servant of Saul, king of Israel, who has been with me for the last one or two years. I have no fault to find with him from the day he gave himself up to me to the present time.' But the Philistine leaders were angry with him. 'Send the man back . . . in case he turns on us once battle is joined. Would there be a better way for the man to regain his master's favour than with the heads of these men here? Is not this the David of whom they sang in the dance:

> "Saul has killed his thousands,
> David his tens of thousands"?'

[1 Sm 29:3-5]

So David returned to Ziklag while the Philistine army marched north to meet Saul. There, on the slopes of Mount Gilboa, Saul saw his sons killed in battle, and as it became clear that the day was lost he asked his armour-bearer to kill him. He was afraid to do so, so Saul committed suicide in the middle of the battle, and his armour-bearer followed his example. The Philistines decapitated Saul's body and nailed it to the walls of Beth-shan, an important town in the Jordan valley just below the Sea of Galilee, where a major trade route crossed, and the head and the armour they displayed round the Philistine cities. Touchingly, the men of the city of Jabesh-gilead marched through the night and rescued the bodies of Saul and his sons from the Beth-shan wall and gave them an honourable burial. It was Jabesh-gilead which Saul saved from the Ammonites when he first proved that he possessed the spirit of Yahweh and emerged from his obscurity.

David heard the news at Ziklag. The young soldier, an Amalekite serving with Saul's army, who brought the report of the death of Saul and Jonathan thought the news would be welcome. He even made out, in his innocence, that he had killed Saul himself when he saw that they were doomed:

'. . . there was Saul, leaning on his spear, with the chariots and the cavalry pressing him hard. Then he turned round and saw me, and shouted to me. I answered, "Here I am." He said, "Who are you?" "An Amalekite" I replied. Then he said, "Stand over me and kill me, for a giddiness has come on me, though my life is wholly in me still." So I stood over him and killed him, because I knew that once he fell he could not

[84]

survive. Then I took the crown he wore on his head and the bracelet on his arm, and I have brought them here to my lord.' [2 Sm 1:6-10]

David and his men mourned until the evening, and then he called the soldier to him again,

David said to the young soldier who had brought the news, 'Where are you from?' 'I am the son of a resident alien,' he answered 'an Amalekite.' David said, 'How is it you were not afraid to lift your hand to destroy Yahweh's anointed?' Then David called one of his soldiers. 'Come here,' he said. 'Strike him down.' The man struck him and he died. 'Your blood be on your own head,' David said 'for your own lips gave evidence against you when you said, "I killed Yahweh's anointed."' [2 Sm 1:13-16]

The movingly beautiful lament of David for Saul and Jonathan follows [2 Sm 1:19-27], and there is every reason to think that it is authentic.

There is no reason to doubt that David's grief was genuine, but it is equally important to notice how cleverly he handled the extremely delicate political situation. This was the moment for which he had waited and prepared; a false move now could have had disastrous consequences. The Israelites were a defeated and divided people. It is doubtful whether the northern and southern tribes had ever been under a single ruler or ever act together as a nation, and no matter how loyal the people in the south might be towards David, the northern peoples would treat him with the deepest suspicion. He was a southerner, their king had denounced him as a traitor, and he was a vassal of the Philistines.

[85]

It says much for David's personality and skill that he finally won them over.

From this point of view, David's reaction to the news of the death of Saul was important; it was essential that the northerners should have no chance of accusing him of rejoicing at Saul's downfall. So as soon as the Judaeans had anointed him king of Judah at the ancient southern sanctuary of Hebron, David sent messengers to the town of Jabesh-gilead:

'May you be blessed by Yahweh . . . for doing this kindness to Saul your Lord, and for burying him. And now may Yahweh show kindness and faithfulness to you! I too shall treat you well because you have done this. And now take courage and be men of valour. Saul your lord is dead, but the House of Judah has anointed me to be their king.' [2 Sm 2:5-7]

The first moves in the creation of the Davidic kingdom were being made. If David had hoped that the union of the people under his rule would come smoothly he was mistaken. Saul's commander-in-chief, Abner, had already had a surviving son of Saul, Ishbaal, anointed king of the northern group. More than seven years were to pass before David became king of the whole people.

The delicate situation broke out into a desultory war, and no doubt the Philistines were glad to let it develop. There was no need for them to station garrisons if the Israelites were fighting amongst themselves. The only significant incident recorded about the fighting was the death of Asahel at the hands of Abner; Asahel was the brother of Joab, David's commander-in-chief, and the personal enmity which sprang up between Abner and

Joab was to prove useful to David later. In the end the solution came not through any military victory but by internal divisions within the northern camp. Ishbaal was a weak ruler and the real power lay with the army commander, Abner. Slowly he played an increasingly arrogant hand, until he ended by taking one of Saul's concubines, a certain sign, in the conventions of the times, that he was stepping into Saul's shoes. Ishbaal objected, and Abner, in angry exchange, threatened to go over to David and take the northerners' loyalty with him: 'May God do this to Abner and more', shouted Abner himself, 'if I do not bring about what Yahweh has promised on oath to David, to take the sovereignty from the House of Saul, and set up the throne of David over Israel and Judah, from Dan to Beersheba' [2 Sm 3:9-10]. Ishbaal was too frightened to reply.

Abner followed up his threat by sending messengers to David, and David agreed to meet him on condition that he first sent his wife Michal, Saul's daughter, back to David. So with the approval and support of the elders of the north, and even of Saul's old tribe of Benjamin, Abner went to meet David at Hebron to tell him that the loyalty of the north was his for the asking. It must have been an agreeable moment for David, but at the point when the negotiations seemed secure at last, David's own chief officer murdered Abner. Revenge was the main motive, for Abner had murdered his brother, but he must also have foreseen that a united kingdom would not have room for two commanders-in-chief. Unknown to David, Joab sent messengers after Abner, and he returned to be murdered by Joab as he passed one of the recesses of the great main gate of Hebron. Once more David had to quickly dissociate himself publicly, for fear that the northerners would think that their negotiator had been killed at his command:

when David heard of this, he said, 'I and my kingdom are innocent for ever before Yahweh of the blood of Abner son of Ner; may it fall on the head of Joab and on all his family! May the House of Joab never lack men with the discharge or the leprosy, or only fit to hold a distaff, or falling by the sword, or short of bread!' [2 Sm 3:28-29]

Abner was given a full state funeral and a period of public mourning: 'That day all the people and all Israel understood that the king had no part in the death of Abner son of Ner' [2 Sm 3:37].

Only Ishbaal stood in David's way now, provided the people could be persuaded to trust David, and this problem was solved by assassination. Two of Ishbaal's own chiefs stole into his room during the afternoon heat, murdered him while he slept and slipped away to David with his head as proof. If they had heard of the fate of the soldier who brought David the news of the death of Saul and Jonathan they might have known what to expect:

'As Yahweh lives, who has delivered me from all adversity, the man who thought to bring me good news when he told me Saul was dead, this man I seized and killed at Ziklag, rewarding him for his good news. How much more when bandits have killed an honest man in his house, and on his bed! Am I not bound to demand account of his blood from you, and wipe you from the earth?' Then David gave an order to his soldiers, who put them to death, cut off their hands and feet, and hung them up beside the Pool of Hebron. Ishbaal's head they took and buried in Abner's grave at Hebron. [2 Sm 4:9-12]

The way was clear; the two men who might have held the loyalty of the northern people lay buried in a royal grave at Hebron, and David had avoided any implication that he was responsible for their deaths. The elders of the tribes of the north came to him at Hebron, entered into an alliance with him and anointed him their king. The full reign of David had begun and the nation had begun its period of political maturity. David and his descendants were to rule over it, or at least part of it, until the blinded Zedekiah and his people were led into exile by the Babylonians, leaving behind them the column of smoke which marked where the Babylonian troops were systematically destroying Jerusalem.

Establishing his capital at Jerusalem was the most astute political decision David ever made. At first sight it had little to commend it; the small narrow city straggled along a narrow ridge with the land falling away at an angle of forty-five degrees; the ridge flattened out at one end to form a gentle hill, but this was the end furthest away from the only water supply, so the houses huddled together along the crest of the ridge and on unstable terraces down its sides. The water of the Gihon spring was at the foot of the ridge, where protective fortifications would be overlooked by the equally steep slopes of the other side of the narrow Kidron valley, yet fortifications there had to be if the town was to survive. The remains of tunnels, shafts, covered pools at the end of conduits, and heavily fortified towers over-looking the spring all testify to the difficulty. But in David's eyes the town had advantages which outweighed all difficulties: it was neutral and it was central. It was still in the hands of Canaanites, the Jebusites who had been in possession when the Israelites arrived in Palestine; and it lay in the central belt of land which separated the territories of the northern and southern groups of Israelite tribes. Neither group would have grounds for fearing political subordination to the other, for the country's capital would have no Israelite political history. Equally important, for the political and the religious are not to be separated, it had no associations with the covenant religion of Israel. The tribes had used Canaanite sanctuaries as central sanctuaries for the Israelite confederation, either by displacing the Canaanite cult or by accepting that the two cults could exist side by side on the same site. So far, the city sanctuary at Jerusalem had never been used by the Yahweh cult; once the sacred Ark had been established there all the people would be able to accept the city as the one central sanctuary.

The text of the account of the capture of Jerusalem in 2 Samuel 5 is too uncertain for a clear reconstruction of the events, but it appears that the Jebusites were so confident of the city's defences that they boasted to David that it could be held against his attack even if the only defenders were the crippled and the blind. But Joab led a party up the town's water shaft (2 Sm 5:8; 1 Chr 11:6), penetrated the defences and opened the way for the city to be taken. It is hard for us to imagine

how small and insignificant the town was, for at the
most it was only four hundred yards long and a hundred
and fifty yards wide, lying entirely outside the present
walls of the Old City, south of the Temple area, on the
Ophel ridge between the Tyropoeon and Kidron valleys.
But it was enough, and David set about making sure of
its fortifications, for the civil war was over, and the
Philistines could no longer ignore him.

The Philistines did not leave him alone for long, but
now David had a fortified base. A Philistine force appeared in the valley south of Jerusalem, but David was
so confident that the city was safe that he attacked the
main Philistine camp about four miles away. It was an
indecisive engagement, and the Philistines moved against
Jerusalem again; this time the job was done properly:

Again the Philistines marched up and deployed in the Valley
of the Rephaim. David consulted Yahweh, who answered, 'Do
not attack them from the front; go round to their rear and
engage them opposite the balsam trees. When you hear the
sound of steps in the tops of the balsam trees, advance, for
that will be Yahweh going out ahead of you to rout the army
of the Philistines.' David did as Yahweh had ordered and
routed the Philistines from Gibeon as far as the Pass of Gezer.
[2 Sm 5:22-25]

It is a pity that no Philistine records have yet been discovered, for it would be interesting to see their view of
their attempts to extend their territory inland. Although
another defeat of them at the hands of David is mentioned, this seems to be the decisive moment when they
were contained in the area along the coast where they

[91]

had first established themselves. The forces they deployed could not have been all that large, for there seems to have been no attempt on their part to set up a serious siege around the thousand-yards length of Jerusalem's wall, but they were the most serious threat the Israelites had to face during these critical years when they were becoming dominant over the Canaanites, and their threat was the direct motive for the establishing of the monarchy in Israel. Once that threat was removed the monarchy was free to turn to the internal development and organisation of the nation. The nation was fortunate to be living in a power vacuum, a brief respite from serious threat, for neither Egypt nor Mesopotamia was concerned to control the area. The vacuum was not to last, but while it was there the nation expanded into it.

You might like to consider: how far a centralised pattern of public worship interferes with individual responsibility in prayer, or is an essential framework without which the individual would find it more difficult to express his relationship with God.

The Crisis of Kingship

ONLY ONE further thing remained to be done for David's kingdom to be as secure in its new unity as human foresight could make it. From the earliest that can be discovered of the Hebrews' consciousness of themselves as a single people, their unity had been expressed through a single central religious symbol: the sacred Ark. The events following its capture by the Philistines had disguised this fact, for the new central institution of the monarchy gave the people a focus for their growing national consciousness. If the Hebrew kings had followed the example of the nations surrounding them, the king would have become the religious as well as the political centre of the country. It is dangerous to generalise about such a complex institution as monarchy, for it took many different forms over such a wide area as the Fertile Crescent, and there was constant change and development in it, but the priest-king was a common form, and even the god-king in Egypt. It is particularly significant, however, that the new capital, Jerusalem, had a tradition of priest-king rule before David captured it. The evidence for this is the strange incident in the book of Genesis when Abraham was met by the king of Jerusalem, who was a priest of the Phoenician cult of El Elyon:

Melchizedek king of Salem brought bread and wine; he was a priest of God Most High. He pronounced this blessing:
> 'Blessed be Abram by God Most High, creator of heaven and earth, and blessed be God Most High for handing over your enemies to you.'

And Abram gave him a tithe of everything. [Gn 14:18-20]

David became the king of Jerusalem; it would be natural for him to continue the Jerusalem tradition of sacral kingship.

But the sacred Ark was the symbol of an entirely different form of government: the confederation of the tribes in which the authority lay with the heads of the families who belonged to the tribes. For all that such a prophet as Samuel is given an important place in the making of the king, it is clear that at this stage in the monarchy it was the people themselves who carried the real authority. 'The men of Judah' anointed David king of Judah (2 Sm 2:4), and 'all the elders of Israel' anointed him king of Israel (2 Sm 5:3). There is a real and fundamental difference here between two forms of kingship: the ancient Canaanite sacral kingship of Jerusalem, and the very new kingship of the Hebrew tribal federation. The tension inherent between these two forms was never to be resolved until the monarchy

itself collapsed, but it was the presence of the sacred
Ark in Jerusalem that preserved the basic Hebraic attitude to government. That attitude rested on the fact that
the nation had been created by the covenant God had
made at the exodus from Egypt, and any form of government had to be subordinate to that covenant.

So it is particularly significant that David moved the
Ark to Jerusalem as soon as he was settled in the new
capital, and that it was moved with complex sacrificial
rites over which David presided:

David . . . went and brought the ark of God up from Obed-
edom's house to the Citadel of David with great rejoicing.
When the bearers of the ark of Yahweh had gone six paces,
he sacrificed an ox and a fat sheep. And David danced whirl-
ing round before Yahweh with all his might, wearing a linen
loincloth round him. Thus David and all the House of Israel
brought up the ark of Yahweh with acclaim and the sound of
the horn. . . . They brought the ark of Yahweh in and put it
in position inside the tent that David had pitched for it; and
David offered holocausts before Yahweh, and communion
sacrifices. And when David had finished offering holocausts
and communion sacrifices, he blessed the people in the name
of Yahweh Sabaoth. [2 Sm 6:12-18]

To preside over sacrifices was no more than the preroga-
tive of the nation's leader in the Hebrew tribal tradition,
but David's actions here are much wider than that, for
he wore the specifically priestly garment of the linen
ephod, and he gave the people the priestly blessing. No
matter how much the editors might have expanded the
details (and there is no reason to think that the account

in 2 Samuel is in any way expanded in the light of later practice—that process occurred with the version given in Chronicles, as a comparison with 1 Chronicles 15 will show), David's actions are priestly in a professional sense. It is legitimate to see here the influence of the tradition of the Canaanite Jerusalem priesthood, and to conclude that David took over that tradition when he took over the city. All the more important was it, then, that the sacred Ark should be there to keep the covenant at the heart of the nation's life.

All that could humanly be done to establish the kingdom had been done, and now David's work was confirmed by God through the prophet Nathan. If Samuel, as he is portrayed in the later accounts, is left out, Nathan is the first of the great line of prophets who were to be consciences to the kings. Fearless and independent, they viewed the events of their times from the point of view of the God of the covenant, and they told the kings what God required of them, no matter what the consequences. Now Nathan came to David to tell him that God had confirmed his reign and would establish it permanently. The covenant people were finally established in the land God had promised to them, and David and his descendants were chosen by God as the chief officers of the covenant:

' "Yahweh Sabaoth says this: I took you from the pasture, from following the sheep, to be leader of my people Israel; I have been with you on all your expeditions; I have cut off all your enemies before you. I will give you fame as great as the fame of the greatest on earth. I will provide a place for my people Israel; I will plant them there and they shall dwell in that place and never be disturbed again; nor shall the wicked continue to oppress them as they did, in the days when I appointed judges over my people Israel; I will give them rest from all their enemies. Yahweh will make you great; Yahweh will make you a House. And when your days are ended and you are laid to rest with your ancestors, I will preserve the off-spring of your body after you and make his sovereignty secure. . . . Your House and your sovereignty will always stand secure before me and your throne be established for ever." ' [2 Sm 7:8-16]

The blessing was confirmed by victories and the extension of the area controlled by David until it stretched from Damascus in the north to Edom in the south, and in both places he installed governors. At the end of 2 Samuel 8 there is a list of the officers of the kingdom: commander-in-chief, recorder, chief priests, secretary, and commander of the mercenaries. It is significant that neither Nathan, nor anyone else, is named as the establishment prophet. There was soon to be urgent need of an independent voice.

The testing moment of David's reign had arrived, just as he seemed most secure, and the threat came from David himself. The king of the Ammonite people, in the semi-desert area to the east of the Jordan valley, died, and David sent ambassadors to express his condolences. The ambassadors were treated as spies, had half of their beards shaved off and their clothes trimmed to expose their buttocks, and were sent back to David. They were too ashamed to return any further than Jericho, the first Hebrew city across the Jordan, and David told them to stay there until their beards had grown again. War was inevitable; the Ammonites strengthened their position by hiring mercenaries from the Armaean peoples to the north and east, but Joab, David's commander, defeated the force by tackling the mercenaries first. When an enlarged and consolidated army of Aramaeans returned David himself went to meet it and won such a decisive victory that there was no danger of the Aramaeans interfering again. Next spring, 'the time when kings go campaigning', David sent a punitive expedition against the Ammonites and it settled down to besiege the town of Rabbah, the modern Amman, capital of the kingdom of Jordan. The siege was in the charge of Joab, David remained in Jerusalem, and one of the officers with the army besieging Rabbah was named Uriah.

Across the flat roofs of the many levels of his congested little capital, David saw Uriah's wife, Bathsheba, bathing. He sent for her and slept with her, and he feared that she was pregnant by him. The scandal of adultery with the wife of a man fighting for him was too large a strain to impose on the newly stabilised and unified state; David sent for Uriah, ostensibly to report on the siege of Rabbah but really to give him the opportunity of spending a night with his wife so that David's child would be attributed to Uriah. Only one factor was missing from David's calculations: he had failed to reckon with Uriah's loyalty towards his fellow officers fighting before Rabbah:

When Uriah came into his presence, David asked after Joab and the army and how the war was going. David then said to Uriah, 'Go down to your house and enjoy yourself.' Uriah left the palace, and was followed by a present from the king's

[98]

table. Uriah however slept by the palace door with his master's bodyguard and did not go down to his house.

This was reported to David; 'Uriah' they said 'did not go down to his house.' So David asked Uriah, 'Have you not just arrived from a journey? Why do you not go to your home?' But Uriah answered, 'Are not the ark and the men of Israel and Judah lodged in tents; and my master Joab and the bodyguard of my lord, are they not in the open fields? Am I to go to my house, then, and eat and drink and sleep with my wife? As Yahweh lives, and as you yourself live, I will do no such thing!' [2 Sm 11:7-12]

David pressed him to stay another night, and that evening he made Uriah drunk, but he still insisted on spending the night in the quarters of the palace guard. The only alternative David could see was for Uriah to die so that he could marry Bathsheba, but it would have to be done quickly. So Uriah carried his own death warrant back with him to Joab in a sealed letter:

Next morning David wrote a letter to Joab and sent it by Uriah. In the letter he wrote, 'Station Uriah in the thick of the fight and then fall back behind him so that he may be struck down and die.' Joab, then besieging the town, posted Uriah in a place where he knew there were fierce fighters. The men of the town sallied out and engaged Joab; the army suffered casualties, including some of David's bodyguard; and Uriah the Hittite was killed too. [2 Sm 11:14-17]

The whole cynical scheme must have been an incredible test of Joab's loyalty to David, and David played it out to the end. Joab had sent many of his men to their deaths to make sure that Uriah was killed, and the man who brought David the news was sent back to Joab with messages of encouragement and consolation:

'Say this to Joab, "Do not take the matter to heart; the sword devours now one and now another. Storm the town in greater force and overthrow it." . . . 'When Uriah's wife heard that her husband Uriah was dead, she mourned for her husband. When the period of mourning was over, David sent to have her brought to his house; she became his wife and bore him a son. [2 Sm 11:7-27]

To David the incident must have appeared over and settled. It fell to Nathan to confront the king with the morality of his act, for the whole future of the kingdom turned on the incident. If the king considered himself above the law, the owner of his subjects and, like any other Canaanite absolute monarch, accountable to no other authority, this would strike at the very heart of the covenant relationship and the sovereignty of God expressed through involvement in every aspect of the lives of his people. At a later stage in the nation's history, when the kings had proved themselves incapable of ruling the people according to the principles of the covenant, the detailed complexity of the law was given divine authority down to the last letter. Rule by regulation replaced personal rule by a king acting in the name of God. It was largely due to Nathan that the failure of personal royal rule did not occur much earlier with David himself, the first effective king.

Nathan was faced with the extraordinarily delicate task of making the king recognise and acknowledge his sin. He approached the problem obliquely, through David's pride in the fairness with which he administered justice in the cases his subjects brought before him. Nathan put a case to David:

'In the same town were two men,
one rich, the other poor.
The rich man had flocks and herds
in great abundance;
the poor man had nothing but a ewe lamb,
one only, a small one he had bought.
This he fed, and it grew up with him and his children,
eating his bread, drinking from his cup,
sleeping on his breast; it was like a daughter to him.
When there came a traveller to stay, the rich man
refused to take one of his own flock or herd
to provide for the wayfarer who had come to him.
Instead he took the poor man's lamb
and prepared it for his guest.'

[2 Sm 12:1-4]

It is the method of parable, which Christ was to use so extensively. A story is told which invites the listener to form a judgment, and he is then shown that the story is parallel to his own situation. David's reaction was exactly as Nathan had expected:

David's anger flared up against the man. 'As Yahweh lives,' he said to Nathan 'the man who did this deserves to die! He must make fourfold restitution for the lamb, for doing such a thing and showing no compassion.'

Then Nathan said to David, 'You are the man. . . .' [2 Sm 12:5-7]

The identification was just; David accepted it penitently and publicly, and the child died. Viewed with the eyes of David's contemporaries, the incident was closed and God's goodwill demonstrated when Bathsheba went on to bear David another son, conceived as he consoled her for her dead child, whom they named Solomon.

Nevertheless, the biblical account gives the firm impression that the high point in David's reign had passed, and from now onwards the king was more and more involved in personal tragedy and national crisis. With the defeat and enslavement of the Ammonites, sealed by the capture of Rabbah, the last external threat to the kingdom was eliminated. There was no longer an outside enemy as a focus for energy and ambition, so the tensions had to find expression within the kingdom's own life. The royal court had been made the centre of that life, and David could not avoid being deeply involved. What began as a family matter spread until it affected the succession to the throne and embroiled the whole kingdom in civil war.

The trouble began amongst David's children, born to him by a number of different wives and concubines. One of the sons, Amnon, raped his half sister, Tamar, who was full sister of Absalom. If David had acted promptly and justly the incident might have gone no further, but Amnon was his eldest son and he allowed him to go unpunished. Absalom decided to revenge his sister. He waited two years for his opportunity, and it came when the royal sons, without David, went to the celebrations accompanying the annual shearing of Absalom's flocks. During the feasting Absalom had Amnon murdered, and then fled to his mother's family to the east of the Sea of Galilee.

Eventually, Absalom was reconciled with David again, mainly through the mediation of Joab, but not until he had endured the humiliation of living for two years back in Jerusalem but unable to share in the life of the court. In the narrow confines of the tiny city he must have found his exclusion from the court intolerable. Yet no sooner was he reconciled with David than he began the intrigues which were to bring about his downfall. Absalom's mother was a northerner, and his estates lay in the northern part of the country, Israel as distinct from Judah, so it was natural that he should set about building up a following amongst the northern tribesmen. He appealed to them at the point where they would feel most in need of help and most concerned with their personal interests—the legal cases brought before the king's court in Jerusalem. Delay in obtaining a hearing, and suspicions of unfairness (and in every case there would be one party dissatisfied with the result) gave Absalom his opportunities:

Absalom procured a chariot and horses, with fifty men to run ahead of him. He would rise early and stand beside the road leading to the gate; and whenever a man with some lawsuit had to come before the king's court, Absalom would call out to him and ask, 'What town are you from?' He would answer, 'Your servant is from one of the tribes in Israel.' Then Absalom would say, 'Look, your case is sound and just, but there is not one deputy of the king's who will listen to you.' Absalom would go on to say, 'Oh, who will appoint me judge in the land? Then anyone with a lawsuit or a plea could come to me and I would see he had justice.' And whenever anyone came up to do homage to him, he would stretch out his hand and take him and kiss him. Absalom acted in this way with all the Israelites who came to the king for justice, and so Absalom seduced the hearts of the men of Israel. [2 Sm 15:1-6]

[103]

After four years of this, Absalom obtained permission to go to the sanctuary at Hebron, where David had been crowned, and there his supporters proclaimed him king.

Clearly the conspiracy was far larger than David had anticipated, and he fled from Jerusalem, across the Jordan, to Mahanaim. Absalom entered the city in triumph and symbolically claimed David's position by publically taking over his father's concubines. If Absalom had pursued David immediately the kingdom would have been his, but he was advised to wait until he had mustered all available forces, and the delay gave David time to gather around him all who had remained loyal to him. The two forces met somewhere to the north of Jerusalem, and at the end of the day David's commanders could report an overwhelming victory to him. But the king had ordered Absalom's life to be spared, an order which Joab had been careful to disobey, and once more David's affection for his own family came near to robbing him of the loyalty of his followers:

The king shuddered. He went up to the room over the gate and burst into tears, and weeping said, 'My son Absalom! My son! My son Absalom! Would I had died in your place! Absalom, my son, my son!' Word was brought to Joab, 'The king is now weeping and mourning for Absalom.' And the day's victory was turned to mourning for all the troops, because they learned that the king was grieving for his son. And the troops returned stealthily that day to the town, as troops creep back ashamed when routed in battle. The king had veiled his face and was crying aloud, 'My son Absalom, Absalom, my son, my son!'

Then Joab went indoors to the king. 'Today' he said 'you

are covering the faces of all your servants with shame when they have saved your life today, and the lives of your sons and daughters, of your wives too and your concubines, all because you love those who hate you and hate those who love you. Today you have made it plain that commanders and soldiers mean nothing to you, since now I see that if Absalom were alive today and we all dead, you would be pleased. Now get up, come out and reassure your soldiers, for if you do not come I swear by Yahweh not one man will stay with you tonight. . . .' [2 Sm 19:1-7]

David hastened to retrieve a situation which could rapidly have developed into national disintegration, and the restoration of his rule took all his skill, for Absalom's chief of staff, Amasa, was only hindered from continuing the rebellion by his swift assassination by Joab, and a dispute between the northern and southern elements in David's forces led to the northern faction being besieged in Abel-beth-maacah, a town in the far north above the Sea of Galilee. Fortunately the townspeople solved the problem by throwing the ringleader's head over the wall to Joab, who then raised the siege.

The struggle for the succession had already been bitter enough to threaten David's own life to the point where he had had to flee from his capital, and the manœuvrings and forming of factions continued as he approached old age. It was inevitably so, for the king was the effective centre of unity, and if his personality was unequal to the task the other national institutions and forces could not bear the strain. This was as true of the national religion as it was of the law or of the prestige and position of Jerusalem. David had centred

[105]

them all on the person of the king, and the older tribal relationships, which had served the nation during the period of settlement, had inevitably become weaker. The king's power touched everyone in the country to some extent, but for the growing band of administrators and officials at court it was a matter of life and death. Whoever succeeded to the throne at David's death would make quite certain that there was no opposition to endanger his position during the critical period of settling down.

The position crystallised into two parties. One consisted of David's son Adonijah, supported by Joab and the only survivor from Saul's massacre of the priests at Nob, Abiathar. The other candidate was Solomon, supported by his mother Bathsheba, Nathan the prophet, and the priest Zadok. It is well worth looking at the membership of these two parties, for it seems very likely that they represented two clearly distinct political groups, formed by the circumstances in which they became associated with David, and with widely differing views about the nature of the monarchy itself.

Both Joab and Abiathar were associated with David before he became king and before the capture of Jerusalem. David made Joab his army commander during the period at Hebron, and, if the account in the Book of Chronicles may be depended on, it was Joab who climbed the water channel through which Jerusalem was captured. Abiathar was the earliest of the priests to flee to David during the time when he was an outlaw flying from Saul. These men belonged to the old Israel, the period of the Judges and of the occupation of the country by the nomads. The tribal organisation was still dominant then, and the tribal values the guide to the people's lives. It was still largely an unstratified society in which the law and the leadership rose naturally from the whole community.

The men in the other party, the supporters of Solomon, emerged at a significantly later time, after the capture of Jerusalem. Nathan at first supported David in his wish to build a temple for the Ark (2 Sm 7:2-3); that same night he found that God did not approve of a temple, and changed his advice, but the earlier suggestion shows how Nathan's mind worked. The building of a temple represented the decisive movement away from the freedom and mobility of the tribal society into the Canaanite pattern of life. So too with the priest Zadok. Zadok is mentioned for the first time, jointly with Abiathar, as one of the two official priests at David's court in Jerusalem (2 Sm 8:17). Too much must not be made of this, but it is worth noticing the connection of the name 'Zadok' with Jerusalem, for the king of Jerusalem who went to meet Abraham was named 'Melchizedek'—a compound of the Hebrew words for king and righteousness, or of 'king' and a divine name, 'Zedek'. It is at least possible that Zadok was connected with the Canaanite sanctuary at Jerusalem, and that both Nathan and Zadok became associated with David as a result of his assumption of the religious functions of the king when he became king of Jerusalem. If this were so, it would provide a clue to the principles which divided the two parties, and account for the strength of the feelings between them. Adonijah represented the old Hebrew society, the community of the desert, while Solomon represented the new city-centred culture which was steadily emerging as the Canaanite agricultural techniques were mastered and men acquired strong and local territorial ties. In any case, when Solomon gained the throne he became a Canaanite king only distinguished from the surrounding kings by his strength and by his adherence to the Hebrew God Yahweh, as we shall see, and even this latter factor was qualified by his tolerance of the multitude of Canaanite gods worshipped by his wives.

Adonijah was Absalom's full brother, and as handsome and ambitious as his brother had been. Like Absalom, he kept the outward pomp of one who expected to inherit the throne. David had not declared himself about his successor, and in the end Adonijah could wait no longer. He called an assembly and began the kind of celebrations which might easily reach their climax with being acclaimed king:

One day when Adonijah was sacrificing sheep and oxen and fattened calves at the Sliding Stone which is beside the Fuller's Spring, he invited all his brothers, the royal princes, and all the men of Judah in the king's service; but he did not invite the prophet Nathan, or Benaiah, or the champions, or his brother Solomon. [1 K 1:9-11]

Nathan and Bathsheba acted swiftly. It was essential that David should declare himself about the succession, and that he should do so in favour of Solomon. Between them they told David of Adonijah's feast:

'he has gone down today and sacrificed quantities of oxen

and fattened calves and sheep, and invited all the royal princes, the army chiefs, and the priest Abiathar; and they are there now, eating and drinking in his presence and shouting, "Long live King Adonijah!" . . .'

Then King David said, 'Summon Zadok the priest, the prophet Nathan and Benaiah son of Jehoiada.' So they came into the king's presence. 'Take the royal guard with you,' said the king 'mount my son Solomon on my own mule and escort him down to Gihon. There Zadok the priest and the prophet Nathan are to anoint him king of Israel; then sound the trumpet and shout, "Long live King Solomon!" Then you are to follow him up and he is to come and take his seat on my throne and be king in place of me. . . .' [1 K 1:25-35]

The first indication Adonijah had of Solomon's victory over them was the noise as Solomon entered the city in triumph, 'The people all followed him up, with pipes playing and loud rejoicing and shouts to split the earth' (1 K 1:40). Adonijah and his followers fled to the safety of the sanctuary at the northern end of the city, where the Ark rested in its tent, and there they grasped the horns of the altar and waited to see what Solomon would do with them.

You might like to consider: whether the possessions, and vested interests, of a religious organisation hinders it in its examination of the situation within which it exists, and prevents it from suggesting policies or criticising actions.

Solomon

THE FUGITIVES had a brief respite, but only until David's death. Possibly his support while he still lived was sufficient to make Solomon feel secure enough, but the dying king himself asked his son to kill Joab and Shimei, both of them supporters of Adonijah. David's request gives us a glimpse of the realities and harsh uncertainty of the king's court; Joab had served David devotedly throughout his adult life, and if he had made as sure as he could that his own position was secure he is hardly to be blamed for it, but David advised Solomon, 'You will be wise not to let his grey head go down to Sheol in peace' (1 K 2:6). Solomon took the advice and Joab was killed at the altar to which he had again fled for sanctuary. Shimei had cursed David publicly when he fled from Jerusalem during Absalom's bid for the throne, but he had pleaded for mercy as David crossed the Jordan again in his victorious return, and David had forgiven him and sworn that he would not harm him. But Solomon was bound by no such oath, and David asked him to see that Shimei was killed: 'I swore to him by Yahweh I would not put him to the sword. But you, you must not let him go unpunished; you are a wise man and will know how to deal with him to bring his grey head down to Sheol in blood' (1 K 2:8-9).

Yet the chief danger to the throne, Adonijah, lived on in his own house in Jerusalem, until Bathsheba took a hand in the matter. At the end of his life David had been served by a young girl, Abishag, 'to wait on the king and look after him; she shall lie on your breast and this will keep my lord the king warm' (1 K 1:2); Bathsheba now reported to Solomon that Adonijah had asked if he might marry Abishag. David had had no intercourse with the girl, but the association had been close enough for her to be considered one of David's wives or concubines, and a request to marry her could be interpreted as a claim to the throne. It all sounds very thin, and there is no knowing whether Adonijah made the request at all, let alone whether he realised the construction which might be put on it, but it was sufficient to secure his death. Abiathar, the priest who had supported Adonijah, was banished to his family estate in Anathoth, a village about four miles to the north of Jerusalem. His was one of the oldest priestly families in the country, directly descended from Eli, and three hundred years later the prophet Jeremiah was born into 'a priestly family living at Anathoth' (Jr 1:1) to be the nation's conscience during the years when the monarchy itself was destroyed by the Babylonians. But that lay in the far future; now 'the sovereignty was securely in the hands of Solomon' (1 K 2:46); with the opposition dead or banished there was nothing to hinder the full flowering of the kingdom of Israel and Judah.

Solomon inherited a throne whose jurisdiction stretched from the headwaters of the Jordan in the north to the beginnings of the Sinai peninsula in the south, and whose influence and control, in varying degrees, extended beyond this nucleus to all the surrounding states by conquest or alliance. The kingdom of Israel and Judah, under David, was about two hundred miles from north to south, and about sixty miles from east to west, but it controlled something like four times this area, and every trade route between Egypt and Mesopotamia passed through territory dominated by the Hebrews. Solomon's policy was one of consolidation, rather than extension, and of the development of the kingdom's internal organisation, rather than the conquest of further territories.

The kingdom's external links were strengthened in two important directions. At some time early in his reign Solomon married a daughter of the Egyptian pharaoh, and so entered into some kind of political alliance with Egypt. Egyptian control at this time extended northwards into the old Philistine territory along the edge of the Mediterranean, and the pharaoh gave Solomon one of the border cities, Gezer, as a dowry for his daughter; the king must have been a figure of consequence for the pharaoh of Egypt to be willing to pay him the compliment of an alliance, even allowing for this being a period of particularly weak Egyptian rule and the end of a dynasty. To the north Solomon strengthened the links

[113]

already established by David with King Hiram of the island stronghold of Tyre; Hiram had sent materials and craftsmen to assist in the building of David's palace, and Solomon continued the association, according to 1 Kings, when he began to build the temple. At this point it is worth remembering that the Books of Kings were written by historians whose chief concern was to show the importance of the temple in the history of the people, so only this aspect of Solomon's relationship with Hiram is mentioned. But Tyre was also the main port of the eastern end of the Mediterranean and the mother city of colonies all round the Mediterranean, including cities as great as Carthage. As such she was one of the ancient world's most important centres of trade and there can be no doubt that she was of great importance to the Hebrew kingdom's economy.

Not that Solomon entirely succeeded in maintaining control over all the areas David had dominated. Damascus, to the northeast, was captured from its Hebrew garrison by an outlaw leader and his followers and was never regained, and with the death of the Egyptian pharoah whose daughter Solomon had married, a new dynasty started which was hostile towards the Hebrew kingdom. The new pharaoh supported an Edomite king who had fled to Egypt as a boy when David had conquered the country; he now returned to the little kingdom at the foot of the Dead Sea, with memories of the massacre by Joab of all the male inhabitants of Edom, and took over control again. Well might the account in 1 Kings report: 'This is where the harm of Hadad comes from: he loathed Israel and ruled Edom' (1 K 11:25). Possibly it was the memory of this, still burning strong, which led the Edomites to help the Babylonians in their destruction of Jerusalem in 587 BC, and in turn inspired the bitterness of the Hebrew psalm against Edom:

Destructive daughter of Babel,
a blessing on the man who treats you
as you have treated us,
a blessing on him who takes and dashes
your babies against the rock! [Ps 137:8-9]

The events of David's reign sometimes left a long shadow trailing behind them.

If David is to be remembered for his military successes and his realisation of the potential of Jerusalem as a capital, Solomon should be remembered as the patient administrator, and it is on this that his reputation for wisdom rests. Under his rule the country was divided into twelve tax districts, each with an administrator appointed from Jerusalem. These men were responsible for raising taxes from their districts, the forced labour for government building works, and the provisions for the army and royal court. The districts into which the country was divided are listed in 1 Kings 4, and it is deeply significant that these divisions cut across the old traditional tribal boundaries; all the organisation of a highly efficient Canaanite state are emerging in this picture of the kingdom under Solomon, and we may perhaps see here the deliberate undermining of the older forces and traditions. Possibly the people were willing to accept the imposition of controls and the loss of local autonomy for the sake of the peace and prosperity it brought, for the historian reports that:

[115]

Judah and Israel lived in security, each man under his vine and his fig tree, from Dan as far as Beersheba, throughout the lifetime of Solomon.

Judah and Israel were like the sand by the sea for number; they ate and drank and lived happily. [1 K 5:5]

And another historian paints an enchanting picture of the effects of it all on the Queen of Sheba:

When the queen of Sheba saw the wisdom of Solomon, the palace he had built, the food at his table, the accommodation for his officials, the organisation of his staff and the way they were dressed, his cupbearers and the holocausts he offered in the Temple of Yahweh, it left her breathless. . . . [2 Ch 9:3-4]

The temple was the chief achievement in a programme of building and fortification whose impressive ruins can still be seen. Much of the building work was the fortification of cities scattered through the country to turn them into strongholds, and such, too, was the tower of the Millo in Jerusalem, probably above the watergate; the rubble of centuries of natural decay and deliberate destruction has washed down the hillside above Jerusalem's main spring and made it impossible to reconstruct the situation there in Solomon's time with any certainty. But there is certainty about the general position of the temple on the flat hilltop at the northern end of the narrow Davidic city, now occupied by the Muslim shrine Al-Haram es-Sharif, the thirty-four acre 'Noble Sanctuary' with the Dome of the Rock mosque and Al-Aqsa mosque standing in the large open space. The Dome of the Rock mosque, as its name implies, stands over a large rock, the top of which breaks through the flooring, and beneath the rock is a cave, roughly thirteen feet square and ten feet high, which is at present entered by eleven steps. Solomon's temple was closely associated with this sacred rock. The biblical traditions about this area associate it with appearance of God to Abraham and to David, for the tradition used in 2 Chronicles 3 (which was written near the end of the Old Testament period) identifies the rock with the mountain on which Abraham was prepared to sacrifice Isaac, and the earlier 2 Samuel 24 states that it was the place where David saw God's angel about to destroy the people of Jerusalem, after killing seventy thousand in the rest of the country, and that David prevented the slaughter from going any further by admitting his sin. It seems more probable, however, that this was the sacred place for the Canaanite city and that David and Solomon took it over when they became kings of the city, just as the infiltrating Hebrews had used existing sanctuaries when they entered the country after the exodus from Egypt. But whatever the origins of the rock's sacred associations, Solomon chose it as the place for his temple. The temple was erected so that the rock was the foundation of the Holy of Holies, or to the westward of the rock so that the rock was immediately in front of the temple's entrance porch and had the altar of sacrifices standing on it. All traces of the temple itself have long since disappeared, so it is no longer possible to say precisely how the temple was situated in relation to the rock.

The temple building was about a hundred and five feet long, thirty feet wide and forty-five feet high, about the size of a village hall but with thicker walls and, of course, a good deal more impressively decorated than the average village hall. It opened at the eastern narrow end, and if one stood outside the entrance and looked towards the interior, the most striking features were two massive bronze pillars, twenty-seven feet high, standing one each side of the vestibule. Mounting the steps into the entrance, one entered a vestibule fifteen feet long ending in a wall pierced by double doors made from olive wood, and through these doors was a room sixty feet long ending in a flight of steps rising about seven and a half feet to a cedarwood screen. This long room was lit by windows high in the walls which illuminated the gold inlays of the cedar panelling; the room contained a square-topped altar, a foot and a half square and three feet tall, for burning incense; a table three feet long, half as wide and a little over two feet high with twelve loaves on it in two rows; and ten candlesticks ranged in two groups of five at the far end. Everywhere there would be the glint of gold—from the candlesticks, the surface of the altar and the table, and from the smaller utensils and implements, censers and incense boats. At the top of the steps at the far end of the rooms were two pairs of double doors piercing the screen, and through the doors (which you would only pass if you were an important priest, and then only rarely) was the Holy of Holies, a room thirty feet square. It was pitch dark, for there were neither windows nor lamps; here it was that the Ark of the Covenant was brought, with its spread-winged cherubim and long carrying shafts on either side of the gold covered chest containing the tablets of the law. The priests who had carried the Ark came back through the doors and the temple became the nation's proof of God's choice of them and of his presence amongst them:

> Now when the priests came out of the sanctuary, the cloud filled the Temple of Yahweh, and because of the cloud the priests could no longer perform their duties: the glory of Yahweh filled Yahweh's Temple.

Then Solomon said:

> 'Yahweh has chosen to dwell in the thick cloud.
> Yes, I have built you a dwelling,
> a place for you to live in for ever.' [1 K 8:10-13]

The outside of the temple had a low building running against the whole wall all around, except for the vestibule walls and, of course, the entrance; this building contained storerooms, and later it was raised by two more stories, also fitted against the temple's main walls. The whole structure stood in an 'inner court', the south wall of which was also the north wall of the royal palace's inner court, and there was an outer court surrounding the inner court on three sides. The king had an entrance straight into the inner court from the palace, and the people entered through the outer court. The inner court had a great bronze basin standing in it, with twelve statues of bulls as its supports, fifteen feet across and seven and a half feet high, which held twenty thousand gallons of water for the ritual purification of the priests, and on either side of the entrance to the temple stood a row of five smaller basins on wheeled stands, each holding about four hundred gallons, ready for the washing of the sacrificial victims.

The building materials used were mainly local stone and bricks; the lower courses of the temple were of stone, and the upper courses of brick secured by wooden frames, similar to the familiar 'half-timbered' old buildings in England, with the brick hidden inside by cedar panelling. The cedarwood was the only substantial import, and this is the significance of the treaty Solomon made with Hiram, king of Tyre, for Tyre was the main source of the cedars for which the Lebanon was famous:

'So now have cedars of Lebanon cut down for me; my servants will work with your servants, and I will pay for the hire of your servants at whatever rate you fix. As you know, we have no one as skilled in felling trees as the Sidonians.' When Hiram heard what Solomon had said, he was delighted. 'Now blessed be Yahweh' he said 'who has given David a wise son to rule over this great people!' And Hiram sent word to Solomon, 'I have received your message. For my part, I will supply all you want in the way of cedar wood and juniper. Your servants will bring these down from Lebanon to the sea, and I shall have them towed by sea to any place you name; I shall discharge them there, and you will take them over. For your part, you will see to the provisioning of my household as I direct.' [1 K 5:20-23]

It is at least possible that there was more to Hiram's involvement in the building of the temple than that of a mere builders' merchant. Tyre itself was the leading city of Phoenicia, and Phoenician temples have been excavated whose plans are similar to Solomon's temple; with the adoption of the Canaanite pattern of kingship it is not surprising that the Canaanite traditions of temple architecture should also be followed. Solomon himself led the dedication ceremonies and offered the sacrifices, and even the much later account of this in 2 Chronicles,

written at a time when only the priests could offer the
sacrifices, states that Solomon took the leading priestly
part in the consecration of the temple, all the more
significant an account because it adds that 'the priests
stood in their places, while the Levites gave praise to
Yahweh . . .' (2 Ch 7:6). It is at points like this that
we can see how close the Hebrews came to a full acceptance of sacral kingship, with its terrible danger that the
king might be worshipped as divine. At certain times of
the year the sun would rise directly between the two
pillars flanking the eastward entrance of the temple, and
perhaps this was the setting for the coronation of the
king, or an annual enthronement ceremony:

'This is my king, installed by me
on Zion, my holy mountain.'
Let me proclaim Yahweh's decree;
he has told me, 'You are my son,
today I have become your father.
Ask and I will give you the nations for your heritage,
the ends of the earth for your domain. . . .' [Ps 2:6-8]

Or again even more powerfully set in the blaze of day-
break:

Yahweh's oracle to you, my Lord: 'Sit at my right hand
and I will make your enemies a footstool for you.'
Yahweh will force all your enemies
under the sway of your sceptre in Zion.
Royal dignity was yours from the day you were born, on the
   holy mountains,
royal from the womb before the dawn of your earliest days.
Yahweh has sworn an oath which he will never retract,

'You are a priest of the order of Melchizedek, and for ever.' [Ps 110:1-4]

It has been estimated that the population at this time, not counting resident foreigners, stood at about three-quarters of a million people. At one time, during the building of the temple, over a hundred and eighty thousand people were involved in forced labour, quite apart from the considerable standing army whose extent may be judged by the size of the barracks and stables that have been uncovered at Megiddo, Hazor, Taanach, Eglon, and Gezer. Despite the great surge of trade with the surrounding countries which developed under Solomon's rule, the financial burden alone must have been a great strain on the people's loyalty, and it was, in fact, one of the overseers of the forced labour gangs who finally led the revolt which destroyed the unifying work of David and Solomon.

The author of 1 Kings, writing after the horrors of the last years of the monarchy and the terrible apostasy which some of the later kings encouraged amongst the people by their example, sees Solomon's decline as a result of the foreign worship he tolerated. Foreign trade depended on foreign alliances, and these were sealed by marriages and concubines in addition to the women whom so powerful and rich a king as Solomon would attract. These brought with them their native worship, and Solomon encouraged them to do so:

King Solomon loved many foreign women: not only Pharaoh's daughter but Moabites, Edomites, Sidonians and Hittites, from those peoples of whom Yahweh had said to the Israelites, 'You are not to go to them nor they to you, or they will surely sway your hearts to their gods.' But Solomon was deeply attached to them. He had seven hundred wives of royal rank, and three hundred concubines. When Solomon grew old his wives swayed his heart to other gods; and his heart was not wholly with Yahweh his God as his father David's had been. Solomon became a follower of Astarte, the goddess of the Sidonians, and of Milcom, the Ammonite abomination. . . . Then it was that Solomon built a high place for Chemosh the god of Moab on the mountain to the east of Jerusalem, and to Milcom the god of the Ammonites. He did the same for all his foreign wives, who offered incense and sacrifice to their gods. [1 K 11:1-8]

At first sight it may seem that there is little difference between using a Canaanite sanctuary, with all its associations, as a site for the worship of Yahweh, and erecting new sanctuaries dedicated to Canaanite gods for the convenience of resident foreigners; yet the distinction has all the divergence in direction of two streams starting from adjacent points—but on either side of a watershed. They grow into rivers which flow in diametrically opposite directions. The main flow of Hebrew religious experience was to be the gradual realisation that Yahweh's power and concern cover all the experiences which lead men to feel for a pantheon of localised and limited gods; Solomon was giving royal approval to the pantheon just at the moment when its worshippers' needs were beginning to find their deeper satisfaction in the worship of the God of the Covenant, One and Universal. The prophets would have to fight their long rearguard action, and the monarchy itself be destroyed, before the right way for the people could be clearly seen; Solomon must bear his measure of responsibility for the four hundred years of confusion which followed his reign.

The kingdom survived in its unity throughout Solomon's reign, but the fragmenting forces were too strong for the weak and inexperienced son who succeeded him. As we have already seen, there were foreshadowings of the trouble to come when one of the royal overseers, Jereboam, led a revolt amongst some of the labourers from the northern part of the kingdom, but Solomon was too strong for them and Jereboam fled to Egypt, where the new pharoah gave him sanctuary. He returned as soon as he heard of Solomon's death, and asked the new king, Rehoboam, to lift some of the burdens the people had found themselves having to bear during his father's reign.

The confrontation took place, significantly, at the great northern sanctuary of Shechem, with all its associations of the solemn renewal—or even of the first solemn forming, according to some scholars—of the covenant with Yahweh when the northern people straggled into the Promised Land from the semi-desert under the leadership of Joshua (see Jos 24). Jereboam, as spokesman for the northern Israelites, put his request, and the king promised to give his answer in three days' time. Meanwhile, the old experienced counsellors who had served under Solomon advised the king to make concessions: 'Act as servant of this people now, they said, humour them, treat them fairly, and they will be your servants for ever.' But Rehoboam was too uncertain of himself, and his own companions urged him to show the people that he was not going to be intimidated by them:

[124]

On the third day all the people came to Rehoboam in obedi-
ence to the king's command. . . . The king, rejecting the advice
given him by the elders, gave the people a harsh answer,
speaking to them as the young men had recommended. 'My
father made you bear a heavy burden,' he said 'but I will
make it heavier still. My father beat you with whips; I am
going to beat you with loaded scourges.' . . . When all Israel
saw that the king took no notice of their wishes, they gave
him this answer:

> 'What share have we in David?
> We have no inheritance in the son of Jesse.
> To your tents, Israel!
> Henceforth look after your own house, David!'
> [1 K 12:12-16]

Rehoboam sent Adoram, one of the oldest of the counsellors, to try to pacify his northern subjects, but even
this was a tactless move, for Adoram had been closely
associated with the imposition of forced labour, and the
Israelites stoned him to death. Rehoboam hurriedly fled
to the safety of Jerusalem before a similar fate overtook
him. It only remained for the northerners to elect Jereboam as their king and the schism was complete. The
glory of the united kingdom and its empire had lasted
a bare seventy years, from the capture of Jerusalem to
the death of Solomon. It was an achievement which the
nation constantly tried to regain for nearly three thousand years, but so far the forces have proved too strong
for it.

In fact the split came along the natural dividing line;
the forces working against the union at the time were
strong ones because they arose from the history of the
people and the natural conditions under which they

were living, and the very methods used to maintain the unity created new tensions. Until the time of David himself there had been no real political unity between the northern and southern groups of Hebrews, and, indeed, not a great deal of contact, for it is at least very likely that the two groups had entered the country at different times and from different directions. Only a vague awareness of distant kinship, and worship of the same God, tied them together under the compelling leadership of David, and once the obvious advantages of unity were outweighed by the weight of the state structure erected by Solomon it became increasingly difficult to hold the people together. Even the agricultural conditions were sufficiently different to make a common calendar difficult; the harvests could differ by as much as a month between the north and the south, so one of King Jereboam's first acts was to move the time of the agriculturally oriented feasts to fit them into the northern agricultural year.

But the main difference between the two groups of people centred on the acceptance of the Canaanite way of life set by the Jerusalem court. In the end the northerners preferred the old social organisation expressed through the federation of tribes with an elected leader and predominantly local religious sanctuaries serving the people of a particular district. The movement of the Ark to Jerusalem and the building of the temple had never fully satisfied the religious needs of people whose loyalties and traditions were expressed within the clan and tribe rather than in the nation. Jereboam revived the importance of the old sanctuaries, particularly of Dan in the far north, and of Bethel on the borders between the northern kingdom of Israel and what was now the southern kingdom of Judah. No doubt it was convenient to have a royal sanctuary at Bethel on the route from the north to Jerusalem, so that the people would have less cause to go up to the temple, and this is the motive put forward by the author of 1 Kings—as we might expect from one whose main interest lay in the temple:

Jereboam thought to himself, 'As things are, the kingdom will revert to the House of David. If this people continues to go up to the Temple of Yahweh in Jerusalem to offer sacrifices, the people's heart will turn back again to their lord, Rehoboam king of Judah, and they will put me to death.' So the king thought this over and then made two golden calves; he said to the people, 'You have been going up to Jerusalem long enough. Here are your gods, Israel; these brought you up out of the land of Egypt!' He set up one in Bethel and the people went in procession all the way to Dan in front of the other. [1 K 12:26-30]

Nor should we readily accept that the golden calves were a return to idolatry; it is much more likely that they were only pedestals indicating the place where the invisible God was present for worship, or at most symbols of his power, just as the temple in Jerusalem contained the bull-horn motif. The Ark itself, after all, was thought of as a base for God's enthroned presence in the temple. Again, it is much safer to see this action of Jereboam's as the inspiration for the tradition of the worship of the golden calf during the stay at Mount Sinai, rather than the other way round. Exodus 32 gives a long account of the people's impatience as they waited for Moses to return from his meeting with God on the mountain, until they could wait no longer and made themselves a golden calf to worship; we must remember that the traditions of the escape from Egypt were never transmitted for merely academic reasons, but always for their relevance to the times and needs of the people who were listening. The incident of the golden calf is an excellent example of the application of the Mosaic faith to a later situation when a powerful example was needed —and far from undermining the force of the Exodus tradition, such use of it only shows how strong the tradition was. Jereboam's motives, and the instincts of his people, were to return to the old ways of life and put the clock back to the times before power became concentrated in the king at Jerusalem. He underestimated the temptations of kingly power, for not only did the nation split again and never regain its unity, but the line of northern kings became every inch as authoritarian and bloody as their southern brethren.

You might like to consider: how far the form of government in a society helps or hinders the religious life of the people.

The Pattern of Redemption

W HEN TALKING about any period of history the problem is always to know where to start and where
to stop; the causes which influence the course of events
are always found to have roots deeper than one expected, and the consequences are still recognisable as
one explores further and further into the future. Wherever the line is drawn there are ragged edges of explanation and the awareness that relationships and situations are being ignored which would probably contribute
to one's understanding of the area under examination.
No resting-point is entirely satisfactory; in order even to
begin to understand the events of the period we have
been examining, the reigns of Saul, David, and Solomon,
it has been necessary to look at far earlier events and
situations, and the effects of their reigns were felt long
after their deaths. It is necessary, therefore, to look
briefly at subsequent events.

The immediate and most striking impression gained

from reading the two Books of Kings is the instability and disorder of the northern of the two kingdoms, Israel, and even when allowance is made for the bias of the southern historians who were mainly responsible for the account, the impression remains. The northern kingdom survived for two hundred years before it was obliterated by the Assyrians; during that period there were nineteen kings, half of whom met violent deaths; five of the kings managed to start dynasties, but even here only two of the dynasties survived beyond the first son. The northern kingdom had rejected the pattern of Canaanite kingship, yet they had not returned to the principles of the old confederation of the tribes, where leaders only emerged when the circumstances required them. For the fact was that the circumstances always required a leader now, and without the stability of inherited kingship that leader was always likely to be displaced by some other strong man or by the whim of the people. Yet the northern kingdom was the stronger of the two: a striking testimony to the weakness of the southern kingdom, Judah. For although Judah had the stability of the Davidic dynasty, which survived right through without break for nearly five hundred years until the exile in Babylon, the kingdom was geographically and economically smaller than its northern brother, and Israel dominated it.

For the first few reigns there was open war between the two countries, and references to it appear regularly: 'Rehoboam and Jereboam were at war with each other throughout their reigns. . . . Abijam and Jereboam were at war with each other. . . . Asa and Baasha king of

Israel were at war with each as long as they lived'
(1 K 14:30; 15:7; 15:16). Finally this gave way to a
time when Judah was clearly subservient to Israel and
possibly, like the Moabites, had to pay tribute; at any
rate, Israel was in a position to make Judah contribute
troops to a punitive expedition. In fact, it was this kind
of military claim by Israel over Judah which in the end
provoked the Judaeans into the terrible action which
brought about the end of the northern kingdom. Israel
tried to force Judah to contribute to an expedition
against the Assyrians, but Judah threw in her lot with
the Assyrians themselves, despite the protests of Isaiah,
and the Assyrians destroyed the northern kingdom (see
2 K 16:5-17:41, and Is 7-8).

The internal struggles between the two kingdoms
were, however, the lesser of the major factors which
terminated the situation which had permitted the rise
of a Hebrew empire. By far the most significant change
was the filling of the power vacuum in the Near East.
Solomon had only been dead for five years when the first
great power stepped back into the area in force:

In the fifth year of Rehoboam, Shishak the king of Egypt
marched on Jerusalem. He took all the treasures from the
Temple of Yahweh and the treasures from the royal palace,
he took everything, including all the golden shields that
Solomon had made; in place of them King Rehoboam had
bronze shields made, entrusting them to the care of the
officers of the guard who guarded the king's palace gate.
Whenever the king went to the Temple of Yahweh, the
guards would carry them, returning them to the guardroom
afterwards. [1 K 14:25-28]

The Egyptian temple of Amon at Karnak contains lists of countries and towns which the pharaohs had conquered, and here Shishak is credited with thirteen towns scattered throughout Israel and Judah, the Jordan valley, the Negev and the country eastwards at least as far as Rabbah-Ammon. Like his predecessors, and later pharaohs, the Egyptian king had marched up the coast road and fanned out through Palestine. The independence of the area had ended.

In the north and east the other great source of political power was wakening from three hundred years of sleep; Assyria rose to strength under the leadership of a succession of great kings and began to force her way along the fertile crescent towards Egypt. By 853 BC she had won a decisive victory over a confederation of twelve Palestinian kings and nothing was to stop her drive through the area until in her turn she was overthrown by a revolt of one of her own provinces, Babylon. At one stage Assyria penetrated into Egypt as far as Thebes itself. With such mighty forces at work the kingdoms of Israel and Judah paled into political insignificance. Thus David and Solomon stand out against a dark background; before them there is only the unimpressive period of the judges and the failure of Saul; after them there is only the disintegration of the united kingdom and the domination of the area by great foreign powers; in such surroundings it is little wonder that David and Solomon shine.

But there was also a great deal that was impressive in its own right. The creation of the kingdom was itself an achievement which introduced a new dimension into the national life and provided a stimulus and opportunity for that life to express itself in new forms. One of those forms was literature; for the first time that we know of amongst the Hebrews serious historical records and accounts of contemporary events were written. Distinctive blocks of literary material emerged, such as the account of David's rise to power, the history of the sacred Ark, the struggle for the succession during the later years of David's reign, and the building of the temple. These blocks were invaluable sources for the 'authors' of the histories as we now have them, and enabled these authors to compile their works by putting existing blocks together in an editorial framework. Most significant of all, and of outstanding importance, it was during this period that most of the material in Genesis 2-11 was written, and the first of the accounts we have of the exodus and covenant, and the events leading up to it. This is theological writing of great power, an exploration of God's redemptive activity set in a context of man's weakness and need, and it provided a view of history which profoundly affected all the other biblical writings.

The personal contributions of David and Solomon must not be dismissed too quickly in the field of literature. It is impossible to say with certainty that any one of the Psalms was written by David himself; many of them belong clearly to later periods, and in any case they are all likely to have passed through several stages of development in the course of the centuries of public liturgical use; but there are fragments and complete works which are almost certainly by David himself, and they are of such calibre that it is easy to see how the tradition of his authorship of the psalms arose. David's lament for Saul and Jonathan is sufficient example:

Alas, the glory of Israel has been slain on your heights!
How did the heroes fall?
Do not speak of it in Gath,
nor announce it in the streets of Ashkelon,
or the daughters of the Philistines will rejoice,
the daughters of the uncircumcised will gloat.
O mountains of Gilboa,
let there be no dew or rain on you;
treacherous fields,
for there the hero's shield was dishonoured!
The shield of Saul was anointed not with oil
but with blood of the wounded, fat of the warriors;
the bow of Jonathan did not turn back,
nor the sword of Saul return idle.
Saul and Jonathan, loved and lovely,
neither in life, nor in death, were divided.
Swifter than eagles were they,
stronger were they than lions.
O daughters of Israel, weep for Saul
who clothed you in scarlet and fine linen,
who set brooches of gold
on your garments.
How did the heroes fall
in the thick of the battle?
O Jonathan, in your death I am stricken,
I am desolate for you, Jonathan my brother.
Very dear to me you were,
your love to me more wonderful
than the love of a woman.
How did the heroes fall
and the battle armour fail? [2 Sm 1:19-27]

Solomon's reputation for wisdom is a more difficult question, for the Old Testament tradition reached the stage where it made him the author of a major movement in literature, the Wisdom Books, much of which clearly dates from the later period when Greek thought was making itself felt after the exile in Babylon. Yet here again there are indications that Solomon played a part, either by his encouragement of sages or by his own achievement, in the early stages of the movement. There are two passages in 1 Kings which lend support to this, even if it is only the support of a tradition flourishing at the end of the period of the monarchy. The first is in the form of a dream in which God tells Solomon to ask for a gift. In his reply, Solomon says:

'Give your servant a heart to understand how to discern between good and evil, for who could govern this people of yours that is so great?' It pleased Yahweh that Solomon should have asked for this. 'Since you have asked for this' Yahweh said 'and not asked for long life for yourself or riches or the lives of your enemies, but have asked for a discerning judgement for yourself, here and now I do what you ask. I give you a heart wise and shrewd as none before you has had and none will have after you.' [1 K 3:9-12]

These are the appropriate gifts for hearing court cases wisely, but later Solomon's wisdom is given a wider content, ranging into the sciences and into proverbs, the pithy sayings found in every nation which are the vehicle for the common experience of the people:

He composed three thousand proverbs, and his songs numbered a thousand and five. He could talk about plants from the cedar in Lebanon to the hyssop growing on the wall; and he could talk of animals and birds and reptiles and fish. Men from all nations came to hear Solomon's wisdom, and he received gifts from all the kings of the world, who had heard of his wisdom. [1 K 5:12-14]

The movement was to develop into the great humanistic writings at the end of the Old Testament period when such books as Job and Ecclesiastes and many of the psalms explored the problems of human existence. By then the traditional answers connecting suffering with personal guilt were proving radically unsatisfactory; there is a strong element of agnosticism springing from the awareness of the limitations of human understanding, yet it is easy to see how this could develop from the practical wisdom of an experienced ruler immersed in the day-to-day problems of administering justice.

The administration of justice by a central authority was itself an important development of this period. There are traces of an office of judge appointed to administer justice for the members of the tribes (as distinct from the 'judge' as a charismatic military leader) during the period before the monarchy was established, but the very fact that the Hebrews were not a unified society was sufficient to prevent such an office from being very effective. While the natural economic unit was the family or clan, and the Hebrews were living in several different kinds of relationship with the Canaanites in different parts of the country, the administration of justice could centre on the head of the family. The unification of the people, the possibility of more uniform social conditions, and the existence of an effective and accessible central authority, all of which arose from the formation of the monarchy, affected the development of the law and the way it was administered.

The earliest laws were expressed in a 'casuistic' form, the 'if a man . . .' construction which is found in a number of ancient legal codes; the background of this is case law based on precedent. Past decisions about similar situations become an expression of the common mind, and since the cases were heard, and the decisions made, in the most public place of the village, control by the commonly accepted standards of behaviour was always present. With the appearance of the monarchy on the scene, and the central administration of justice, it was at least possible that both the way in which law was formed, and the standards operating in its administration, might change. An indication of this change can be seen in the change of form from the 'casuistic' to a form of direct command: 'you must not . . .', which has been called 'apodictic' law. This directly authoritarian form of the law reflects the central authority of the king and of the priests and lawyers attached to the royal court. Fortunately, the scribes who made the collections of laws in the Old Testament often copied the laws in the form in which they found them, instead or rewriting them in a uniform style, so it is possible to recognise laws belonging to different periods of the nation's development. Exodus 20:22-23:19 is worth reading with this in mind, for this is probably the oldest single collection of laws in the Old Testament, and the differences of form are easily recognisable.

With the disruption of the kingdom the law and its administration remained in the hands of the kings, until they showed that they were incapable of administering it justly. There had always been a close connection between the covenant—the experience of a special relationship between God and the Hebrew nation—and law, for the God with whom the people had entered into covenant was a God who required this relationship to be expressed in the people's dealings with each other. If the law, or the administration of it, departed from the principles of the covenant, then the law or its administration had to change. It was not an easy process, for authority rested with the king even when he was corrupt, so change was slow and dangerous, but when it came it was decisive.

Law had passed from the hands of the people into the hands of the king. When the kings proved that they could not be trusted with it, the law was lifted out of their hands and given divine authority. The process can be seen at its clearest in the formation of Deuteronomy and the part it played in the reform of 622 BC. The whole body of law was put into the mouth of Moses, the spokesman of God, and set in the context of the exodus from Egypt and the making of the covenant. It is an extremely effective literary device, for it brings to bear on the needs of the contemporary society the principles of the experience from which the national life drew its strength; if we keep this purpose in mind, that the lawyers were bringing the covenant to bear on the needs of their own times, we are less likely to make the mistake of judging the lawyers by the standards of modern historical writing.

The centralisation of the law might be safe in the hands of a David or a Solomon, but later kings proved how far power can corrupt. In the period before the monarchy the Hebrew society was still unstratified, and the controls which operated were the natural ones of the family and the small community in which it was comparatively easy for everyone to make his needs known and his opinions felt. With the rise of kings and of royal officials dependent on the king for their position and, indeed, their lives, a new form of control had to emerge. It could not be provided easily by the priests, for they too were closely associated with the royal court, so a new figure emerged, the prophet. Nathan, who successfully rebuked David, was the first of the great line of men who were prepared to withstand the king and, if necessary, the whole of the religious establishment, when they departed from the principles of the covenant. Elijah and Elisha belong to this tradition, and then the succession of men whose teaching has been preserved in their writings or the records of their teaching: Amos, Hosea, Isaiah, Micah, Zepaniah, Jeremiah, Nahum, Habakkuk, and Ezekiel.

These prophets were essentially men who examined their own times and their own society, who saw things from God's point of view and brought the covenant experience to bear on their situation, so that, through them, there was a steadily expanding exploration of the implications of the covenant. This constant process of exploration, and of application of the insights obtained to society, was the main factor in the development of Hebrew religion from its beginnings in the exodus from Egypt to its full flowering towards the end of the exile in Babylon and in the years immediately after it. God's revelation of himself, and the experience of exploring the revelation, occurred within the context of a society with complex society structures and institutions, and within the circumstances of that society's history. The consequences of the covenant had to be worked out for the relationships within the Hebrew society and for its external relationships with other peoples; the greater part of this work was carried out within the structure of the monarchical society whose pattern had been established by the work of David and Solomon. Consequently there is nothing that lies outside the scope of the prophets' scrutiny; the God of the covenant is concerned with the whole of human life in both its corporate and individual aspects, so the prophets examined and judged social injustices, national policy towards other countries (particularly the great powers), the use of the royal power, and the effectiveness of the forms of worship through which the people expressed their relationship with their God. It was inevitable that the monarchy should emerge and develop, but the criterion of its success must always be whether king and people expressed the covenant:

Sons of Israel, listen to the word of Yahweh,
for Yahweh indicts the inhabitants of the country:
there is no fidelity, no tenderness,
no knowledge of God in the country,
only perjury and lies, slaughter, theft,
adultery and violence, murder after murder. . . .

Listen to this, priests,
attend, House of Israel,
listen, royal household,
you who are responsible for justice. . . .

Put the trumpet to your lips
like a watchman on duty at the house of Yahweh,
because they have violated my covenant
and rebelled against my Law.

[Ho 4:1-2; 5:1; 8:1]

Disillusionment with the monarchical society as an expression of the covenant community finally led to the yearning for a new initiative by God, a new relationship between him and his people, a new covenant which would transform men's lives. It would not be at the mercy of human weakness and the failures of human leadership, but would be some form of direct divine rule, bringing a lasting peace, security, and justice:

For there is a child born for us,
a son given to us
and dominion is laid on his shoulders;
and this is the name they give him:
Wonder-Counsellor, Mighty-God,
Eternal-Father, Prince-of-Peace.
Wide is his dominion
in a peace that has no end. . . .

[Is 9:5-6]

Yet the model for this, the person men turned to when they wished to express their yearning for a messiah, was David; such was the impression he made:

A shoot springs from the stock of Jesse [David's father],
a scion thrusts from his roots:
on him the spirit of Yahweh rests,
a spirit of wisdom and insight,

[141]

a spirit of counsel and power,
a spirit of knowledge and of the fear of Yahweh.

[Is 11:1-2]

The messianic community will be a kingdom, and Jerusalem will be the capital of it. This is taken for granted; it is the main proof of the greatness of the men who created the kingdom.

At the centre of Judaism, and of Christianity, there is the claim that God reveals himself in history, not by an occasional intervention in affairs and interference with the course of events, but by his complete involvement in the whole historical process. He is the ground of all that exists, the context within whom everything happens, the source from whom everything comes and the end towards whom all is moving. And he has revealed the pattern of history and given us the key to the understanding of it in the incarnation, the life and work of Jesus Christ:

He has let us know the mystery of his purpose,
the hidden plan he so kindly made in Christ from the beginning
to act upon when the times had run their course to the end:
that he would bring everything together under Christ, as head,
everything in the heavens and everything on earth.

[Ep 1:9-10]

The pattern is one of life out of death, of redemption from hopeless captivity, of resurrection from the extremes of dereliction and death. If this is so, the pattern of historical development is not a simple straight line, but something much nearer the Greek belief in recurring cycles; yet the cycles do not come back to the point from which they started, rather it is the progression of the rising spiral staircase or, perhaps a better image, of a wave motion in which the troughs are as much part of the advance as the peaks. At the exodus the people were raised from the humiliation of slavery into the freedom and privilege of the covenant; from the humiliation of Philistine domination in the Promised Land David won the people their freedom again and created the national state; at the lowest moral point in the degeneration of the monarchy, during the long reign of Manasseh and the submission to the Assyrians, the work of the deuteronomic lawyers provided Josiah with the inspiration to bring the people back to their loyalty to the covenant; and out of the exile in Babylon the voice of the second Isaiah proclaimed the release of the captives without ransom or indemnity:

I am Yahweh, unrivalled,
I form the light and create the dark.
I make good fortune and create calamity,
it is I, Yahweh, who do all this.
Send victory like a dew, you heavens,
and let the clouds rain it down.
Let the earth open
for salvation to spring up.
Let deliverance, too, bud forth
which I, Yahweh, shall create. [Is 45:6-8]

In the covenant relationship the heart of the matter is the pattern of divine initiative and free human response; divine generosity and human dependence; God's steadfast love and the love this creates in man for man to

[143]

give to God again. Whenever mankind has relied on its own powers, or a people has tried to compete with the world on the world's terms and by the world's standards, it has led to chaos and suffering until the lesson of mankind's need for God is again learned and the pattern of the cross and resurrection once more recognised in the contemporary situation. This pattern is the criterion by which we evaluate the work of the men who founded the Hebrew kingdom three thousand years ago; it enables us to look beneath the surface crudities and see the motives of men who tried to express the covenant in their contemporary political institutions, who genuinely tried to mediate God's rule to their people, and in so doing helped to prepare for the birth of Christ.

You might like to consider: whether the messianic hopes of the Jews have been recognisably fulfilled in the church.

THE PATTERN OF REDEMPTION

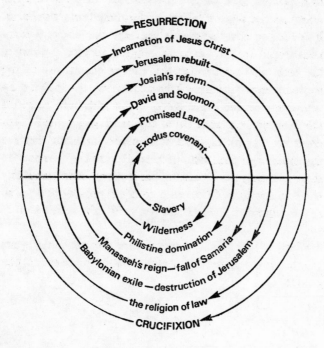

RESURRECTION

Incarnation of Jesus Christ

Jerusalem rebuilt

Josiah's reform

David and Solomon

Promised Land

Exodus covenant

Slavery

Wilderness

Philistine domination

Manasseh's reign—fall of Samaria

Babylonian exile—destruction of Jerusalem

the religion of law

CRUCIFIXION

Index of Names and Subjects

Abraham, 8, 94, 116

Absalom, 30, 102-105, 108, 111

anointing, 63, 68, 81, 85, 89, 94, 109, 134

Ark, 31-32, 36, 47, 54-56, 58, 60, 76, 90, 93-96, 99, 107, 109, 118, 126, 133

Assyrians, 1, 2, 11-13, 59, 130, 132, 143

authority, 29-30, 92-93
  charismatic, 47, 51, 64, 137
  institutionalised, 64, 136
  of king, 80-81, 100, 105-106, 137-138

Babylon, 12, 115, 132
  exile in, 23, 24, 36, 89, 112, 130, 134, 139, 143

Benjamin, tribe of, 43, 45, 48, 62, 63, 75, 87

Canaanites, 12, 13, 16, 17, 18, 19-21, 90
  social structure of, 18, 28
  religion of, 21, 34-38, 41

Christ, 4, 101, 142, 144

community, 28, 61-62, 64, 107
  and government, tensions between, 3, 64, 125-126, 137

covenant, 4, 30, 36, 42, 47, 48, 52, 64, 67, 90, 95-97, 100, 123, 124, 133, 138, 139, 140, 141, 143-144

David, 1, 2, 3, 4, 7, 10, 18, 21, 28, 35, 52, 56, 57-58, 69-74, 75-82, 83-91, 93-109, 111, 112, 114, 115, 117, 122, 125, 126, 127, 129, 132, 133, 138, 139, 140, 141, 143

Egypt, Egyptians, 1, 2, 7-11, 12-13, 14, 15, 16, 17-18, 25, 26, 33, 38, 52-53, 92, 113-114, 131, 132

exile, 23-24, 36, 89, 112, 130, 135, 139, 143

exodus, 10, 23-27, 33, 34, 38, 39, 41, 47, 95-117, 128, 133, 138, 139, 143

Family, Hebrew, 27, 29, 31, 94, 136, 139
  equality in, 27-29

fertility cults, 35, 37, 41, 52

Government, 51, 94-95, 106-107, 115
  and community, tensions between, 64, 125-126, 137
  charismatic, 64, 69
  problems of, 3, 65-66

Hebrews, 1, 7, 8, 9, 10, 12-13, 14, 15, 17, 18, 83
  and native religions, 21, 34-38
  community life, 25, 107

family life, 27, 28, 29-30, 94, 136, 139
religious experience of, 25, 31, 123
national unity of, 18, 66-67, 85, 89, 93-95, 105-106, 125-127, 128, 132-133, 143
Hebron, 78, 86, 87, 88, 89, 104, 106

Israel, northern kingdom (*see also* Judah), 29, 37, 47, 58, 85, 87, 94, 99, 103, 113, 116, 125-128, 130-131, 132

Jerusalem, 7, 15, 21, 35, 46, 56, 75, 89-91, 103, 105, 107, 115, 116, 124, 126, 127, 131, 142
destruction of, 23, 43, 59, 115
Jezreel, 5, 6, 44, 49
Joab, 86-87, 88, 90, 98-99, 100, 102, 104-105, 106, 111, 114
Jonathan, 65-66, 71, 72, 73, 84-85, 88, 134
Josiah, 37, 43, 59
Judah, southern kingdom (*see also* Israel), 27, 45, 46-47, 48, 56, 59, 81, 86, 87, 94, 99, 103, 113, 116, 126-128, 130-131, 132
judge, 30, 47, 48, 132, 136

Kingdom (*see also* Israel, Judah), 85, 132, 137, 142
of David, 7, 75, 86f., 93f., 100
of Solomon, 6, 7, 113f., 124
united, 93, 105, 124, 136-137
disintegration of, 47, 125-128, 137
kingship (*see also* anointing, monarchy), 4, 68, 80-81
Canaanite, 18-19
sacral, 93-95, 107, 120-121

Law, 27, 28, 29-30, 33-34, 47, 100, 105-106, 137-138, 141
Decalogue, 32, 34
Deuteronomic code, 39, 42-43
liturgy, 4, 31, 38-39, 95, 120-121, 133

Megiddo, 5-6, 9, 15, 44
Melchizedek, 94, 107, 122
Mesopotamia, 5, 11-12, 13, 92, 113
Messiah, 69, 142
monarchy (*see also* kingdom, kingship), 27, 30, 56, 57, 92, 93, 100, 122, 137, 141, 143
anti-royalist tradition, 58-61
pro-royalist tradition, 58, 61-63
Moses, 24, 32, 33, 128, 138

Nathan, 28, 96-97, 100-101, 106, 107, 108-109, 139
nation, 18, 67, 85, 89, 93-95, 125-126, 128, 143
nomads, 13, 26, 29, 30, 33, 50, 66, 106

Passover, 31, 38
Philistines ('people of the sea'), 9, 12, 35, 45, 46, 52-56, 60, 62, 64, 65, 66, 68, 70-71, 72, 73, 76-78, 81-84, 85, 86, 91-92, 93, 113, 143
priesthood, 31, 46, 93-94, 95-96, 107, 121-122, 137, 139
prophet, 4, 29, 37, 58, 60, 94, 97, 112, 139-141

Redemptive activity, 4, 133, 142

Sacrifice, 31, 34, 37, 38, 52, 66, 95, 119
Samuel, 19, 57, 58, 60, 61, 63, 66, 67-68, 69, 82-83, 94, 96
sanctuary, 36, 46, 47, 55, 60, 63,

76, 78, 86, 90, 104, 107, 109, 117, 123, 124, 126

Saul, 1, 13, 18, 47, 56, 57, 61, 62, 63, 64, 65, 66-69, 70, 71-73, 75-85, 86, 106, 129, 132, 134

Shechem, 36, 43, 51, 124

Shiloh, 36, 55, 60, 76

Solomon, 1, 2, 3, 4, 6-7, 10, 18, 19, 47, 58, 102, 106, 107, 108, 109, 111-126, 129, 131, 132, 133, 135-136, 138, 140

Temple, 7, 37, 59, 91, 107, 114, 116-122, 127, 131, 133

tribe, tribal society, 18, 25, 26, 27, 46-47, 51, 89, 106-107, 126, 130

Wisdom, 4, 115, 135-136

worship (*see also* liturgy), 31, 34, 36, 122f., 140

Yahweh, power of, 41, 55, 123 spirit of, 48, 62, 63, 69, 84